Origami Instruction Book for Kids Complete Collection

Easy Japanese Origami + Animals Edition

Origami

Ben Mikaelson

Table of Contents

Origami Instruction Book for Kids Complete Collection 1

Table of Contents 3

Origami for Kids 6

Introduction 7

Chapter One: What Is Origami? 9

Chapter Two: Getting Started 13

Chapter Three: Symbols 17

Chapter Four: An Easy Heart 19

Chapter Five: A Cup 26

Chapter Six: A Letter 33

Chapter Seven: A Cicada 40

Chapter Eight: A Bird 47

Chapter Nine: A Little Boat 55

Chapter Ten: A Headfish 62

Chapter Eleven: A Peacock 70

Chapter Twelve: A Fox Face 76

Chapter Thirteen: A Cat 82

Chapter Fourteen: A Tulip 91

Chapter Fifteen: A Whale 99

Chapter Sixteen: A Brachiosaur 105

Chapter Seventeen: A Crane 113

Final Words 128

Origami Instruction Book for Kids Animals Edition 131
Introduction 132
Chapter 1: All About Origami 134
Chapter 2: What You'll Need 137
Chapter 3: How to Make a Square from a Rectangle 140
Chapter 4: A Few Folds 142
Chapter 5: Symbols for Getting Started 153
Chapter 6: Tiger (Face) 155
Chapter 7: Pig (Face) 162
Chapter 8: Bulldog (Face) 167
Chapter 9: Fish 173
Chapter 10: Owl 179
Chapter 11: Bat 186
Chapter 12: Bear Cub 192
Chapter 13: Lion 202
Chapter 14: Penguin 211
Chapter 15: Platypus 217
Chapter 16: Gorilla 226
Chapter 17: Swan 235
Chapter 18: Giraffe 241
Chapter 19: Squirrel 248
See You Soon! 257

© Copyright 2018 - All rights reserved.

It is not legal to reproduce, duplicate, or transmit any part of this document by either electronic means or in printed format. Recording of this publication is strictly prohibited.

Origami for Kids

Easy Japanese Origami Instruction Book for Kids

Ben Mikaelson

Introduction

Congratulations on purchasing *Origami For Kids: Easy Japanese Origami Instruction Book for Kids!*

You'll quickly find this is the best, easiest-to-understand introduction to the ancient Japanese art of paper folding.

There are lots of books on origami. If you visit a bookstore or search online, you'll find hundreds of them—maybe even thousands! But this book is different. This book was written with *you* in mind: you want to know about origami—what it is, where it came from, and how to do it—but you find most of the books on this subject confusing and hard to understand (and maybe even a little boring). But this book will take you by the hand and lead you step by step through 14 different origami patterns. Each pattern has helpful pictures and clear instructions to guide you. You won't be alone, and you won't get lost.

The first ones are *super*-easy. You'll be amazed how quickly you learn to fold simple, square pieces of paper into things that everybody will recognize: cats, boats, birds—even a dinosaur! As you make your way through the book, the patterns will become more challenging and you'll learn new techniques. By the time you finish *Origami For Kids: Easy Japanese Origami Instruction Book for Kids*, you'll not only be impressing your family and friends with your new-found paper-folding skills, but you'll also be amazing them with your knowledge of

Japanese culture and history. You'll not only learn Japanese words, you'll learn how to draw a few of them in the Japanese language. And along the way, you'll discover things you never knew about foxes, peacocks, and many other creatures that have a connection to Japanese culture.

Let's turn the page, then, and travel back in time. We're about to find ourselves 400 years in the past, in Edo, Japan…

Chapter One: What Is Origami?

Before we start looking at origami patterns and folding paper, we need to learn what origami is and where it came from.

We live in a big, beautiful, round world that's full of people who speak different languages and enjoy different customs. Every once in a while, though, a custom from one country becomes very popular in *every* country. That's what happened with origami.

The word *origami* is a Japanese word that means "folding paper." Did you know that paper was invented over 2,000 years ago? We're so used to having paper in our lives every day that we can't imagine a world without it. But paper hasn't always existed. Instead of writing on paper, people would write on other things, like big stone tablets or even dried animal skins. In China and other parts of Asia, people would write on bamboo. But just over 2,000 years ago, a Chinese man named Cai Lun invented paper—or something very close to it. Hundreds of years later, another Chinese man, Ts'ai Lun, invented a type of paper that was much closer to the kind of paper we use today.

Legend has it that, one day, Ts'ai Lun watched a wasp making its nest by chewing up pieces of bamboo, mixing them with its own saliva and then working the whole mess into a flat sheet with its feet. The wasp then used the sheet to build a wall in its nest. Ts'ai Lun copied the wasp, making a paste of bamboo and water and spreading the flat sheet to dry in the sun. Knowledge of his work spread slowly, first to the Middle East, and then, much later, into Europe.

Origami first became really popular in the Japanese city of Edo, which today is called Tokyo and is the capital of Japan. Paper was expensive and not available to most people. Paper and paper folding was limited to religious rituals and formal ceremonies. But over time, as paper became cheaper to make, the people in Edo began to have fun folding paper into shapes that looked like animals, flowers, and insects. They called this art *origami*—"folding paper"—and it quickly became very popular. People would make origami butterflies and use them as wedding decorations. They would attach origami to gifts, like we do today with greeting cards. Instead of a card, people would receive an origami bird or flower.

The idea is really very simple: take a flat, square sheet of paper and make it into a kind of sculpture by folding and bending it in creative ways. There are only a small number of basic origami folds, but the amazing thing about origami is that the folds can be combined in a lot of different ways to make really beautiful designs. The best-known origami design is the Japanese crane, which is a pretty bird very common in Asia. And guess what? You're going to learn how to make an origami crane! You will follow a pattern that is 400 years old!

Origami's Influence

It is easy to make the mistake of thinking that origami is simply a pastime, or even something silly. Because the truth is, origami has had a significant impact on how our technology has helped us. Would you believe that origami has influenced how we build cars? It has! Think of the airbags in the steering wheel and dashboard of your family's car. How did people ever figure out how to stuff such big airbags into those little spaces? That's right: they studied origami. And have you ever seen those huge mirrors and solar panels on space stations? How did the astronauts ever figure out how to get those huge things into such small spaceships? Yes, that's right: they studied the principles of origami.

Origami has had an influence on:

- How we build cars

- How we build microscopes

- How we do heart surgery

- How we build robots

Origami isn't just fun, it can actually help us. Doing origami on a regular basis has been proven to help students become more focused, coordinated, and better at math.

But most of all, making origami is just plain fun.

So what does it take to do it?

Origami designs begin with a square sheet of paper. It can just be plain white paper, it can be colored, or it can even have different colors, prints, and patterns on each side. It's up to you, whatever you want. You can use a small square piece of paper or a big one. Again, it's up to you. Be creative!

People sometimes use scissors when doing origami, but a lot of people prefer to simply fold their paper and not use any other tools. That's what we'll be doing in this book. You won't have to use scissors for any of the patterns you see.

Before we move on to the next chapter, I want to show you something that's pretty cool:

Do you know what that is? That's the word *origami* in traditional Japanese letters. You might want to take some time and learn how to draw it. Then you can show your friends that you not only know how to make origami, you also know how to write it in Japanese!

Chapter Two: Getting Started

Thankfully, you don't need many supplies to practice origami. In fact, you should be able to find most of it around your home. It is this simplicity that makes origami such an enjoyable craft—you can make it from almost any paper and you can do it almost anywhere: on the school bus, at the library, or even camping in a tent. If you have paper with you, there's an excellent chance you can make some origami with it.

Some people think that you need expensive and hard-to-come-by origami paper, a guillotine to cut it with, and something called a "bone folder," which helps make sharp folds and creases. It's called a bone folder because it is traditionally made from a bone, but today, most of them are plastic. You really don't need any of these things, especially when you're just starting out. All you need is a piece of paper and the ability to use your hands.

Of these things, the most likely for you to think you need is origami paper. However, you do not really need special paper any more than other special tools. I recommend starting with only the paper you need, and as your interest and skill expands, you can invest in more. If all you have nearby is a notepad, then use that. If all you have is a newspaper, use that. For simple folds, copy paper works very well. It keeps a crease, doesn't easily wrinkle, and, best of all, you can find it pretty much everywhere. The only requirement is that the paper needs to be square. That means that if you use, for example, a piece of notebook paper, you'll need to cut or tear it into a square.

There is special paper that's already made for origami called *kami*, which is the Japanese word for paper. It's usually colored on one side and white on the other, but sometimes it has bright colors on both sides. Kami is usually inexpensive and is very good for beginners. It holds a crease very well (which is important in origami, as you will soon see); it's not expensive; and it comes in lots of colors.

There is also another type of origami paper called *tant*. It is stiffer than kami and comes in bigger sizes. But it also tears easily, and only comes in solid colors. This means that kami is probably the best choice for beginners. I recommend that you visit a craft or arts supply store; you'll find lots of different paper made just for origami and can choose what's best for you.

Other Supplies?

You won't need scissors for any of the patterns in this book. What you *might* want, however, are some magic markers. For example, in this book you'll be making an origami cat face, and you can make it extra cute by drawing some whiskers on it with a magic marker. And if you want to make it extra *extra* cute, you can get a pack of googly eyes at the craft store when you buy your paper.

Take a look at the origami cat face you're going to make in this book:

If you're very artistic and want to have some fun, you can draw those eyes on your cat face yourself. But if you prefer, you can get a pack of googly eyes at the craft store and stick them to your origami. The googly eyes will shake and roll around and make your cat look funny and alert. Some of the googly eyes you can buy in the craft store have sticky backs; some don't. Just in case your googly eyes don't already have glue on them, you might also want to get a glue stick while you're at the craft store.

Checklist

What do you need to start? Here's a handy checklist:

- Square paper

- Magic markers (optional)

- Googly eyes (optional)

- Glue stick (optional)

- Enthusiasm (this is the most important requirement!)

Once you have everything you need, turn the page and learn how to read the symbols you'll see in the patterns. (Don't worry, there are only a few and they're easy to remember.)

We're almost there…

Chapter Three: Symbols

This book has lots of pictures to help you make origami. The pictures are clear and are sometimes all you will need to complete the project. The written instructions are easy to follow, too. But the pictures do contain some symbols that you might be seeing for the first time, so I want to make sure you understand what they mean.

Take a look at this picture:

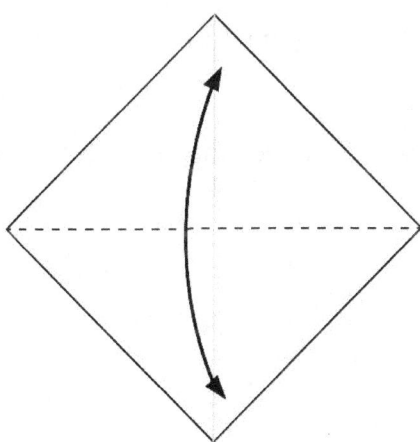

The dotted line shows you where you should fold and unfold.

The arrows show you the direction to fold the paper.

The solid gray line shows you where the crease should be.

Now take a look at this picture:

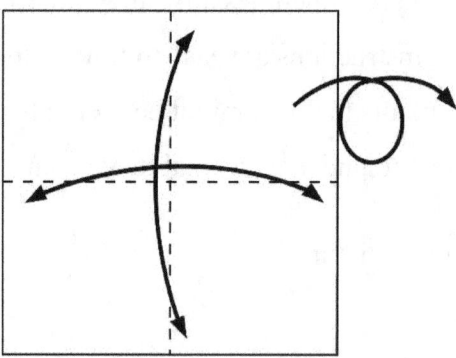

If you see an arrow that loops, it means you should turn the paper over.

And that's it! (See? I told you they were easy to remember.)

Don't worry if you forget them. The instructions for each pattern are easy to understand, and I'll refresh your memory along the way. But if you ever need to study them, the symbol pictures will always be here in Chapter Three for you to study.

Time to Begin!

Are you ready? You're about to start a journey and learn an ancient art. You now have everything you need. There's no need to wait any longer—let's go!

Chapter Four: An Easy Heart

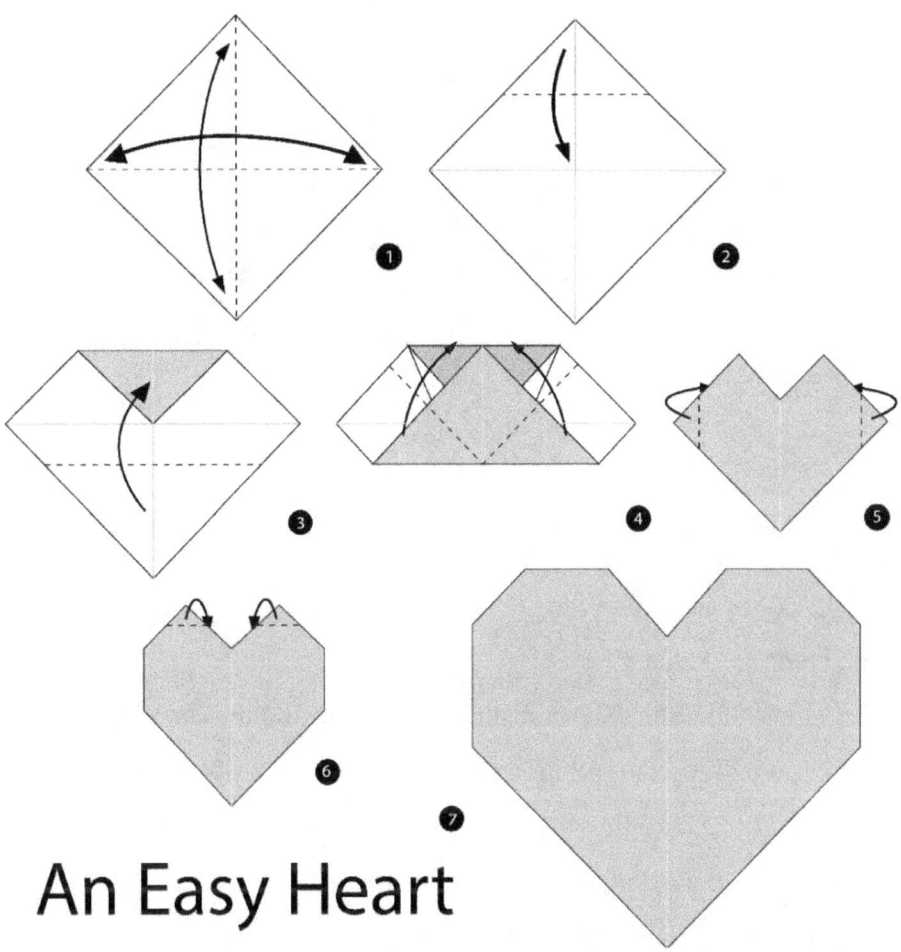

An Easy Heart

Alright, let's get going with something easy, but also exciting and beautiful: a heart!

This origami needs only a few basic folds and is a good introduction to the step-by-step method of this book.

Step 1

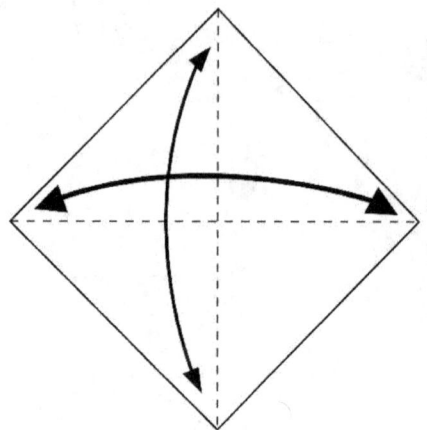

As you can see in the picture, **Step 1** is very easy. All you have to do is make two simple folds.

Fold #1: Take two opposite corners and fold the square piece of paper in half; then unfold the paper.

Fold #2: Take the *other* two opposite corners and fold the paper in half again; and again, unfold the paper.

Congratulations! You've just taken your first step into the world of origami!

Step 2

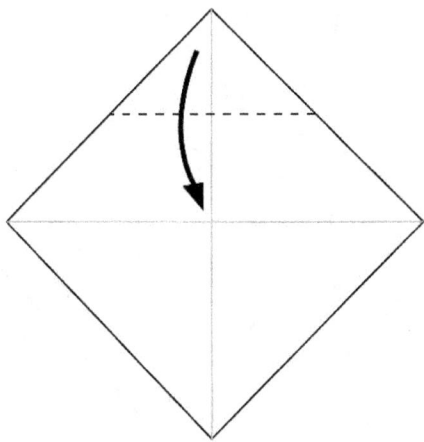

Place your paper flat on the table with one of the corners pointing away from you. (Do you see the solid gray lines in the picture? You should have creases in your paper where the gray lines are.)

Now, fold that corner down so that its point touches the center of the paper. See? Just like in the picture.

Step 3

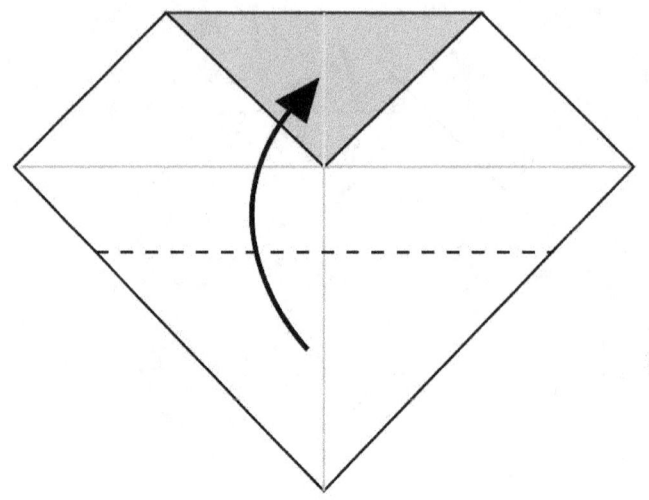

Now you're going to take the point of the *bottom* corner and bring it up so that it touches the very top of the fold you just made. Don't stop at the center of the square but go all the way to the other side. Once the bottom corner is even with the other side, make a fold.

Step 4

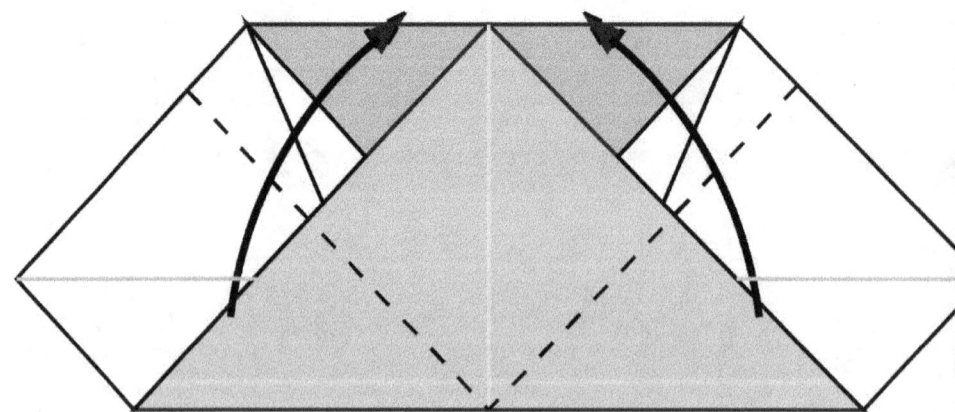

This step might look complicated, but it's actually very simple. You're going to make two diagonal folds here—one on the left and one on the right. Fold each side up toward the center and top of the paper. Follow the picture and it'll be perfect.

(Remember: the solid gray lines show you where the creases are. The dotted black lines show you where you should fold.)

Step 5

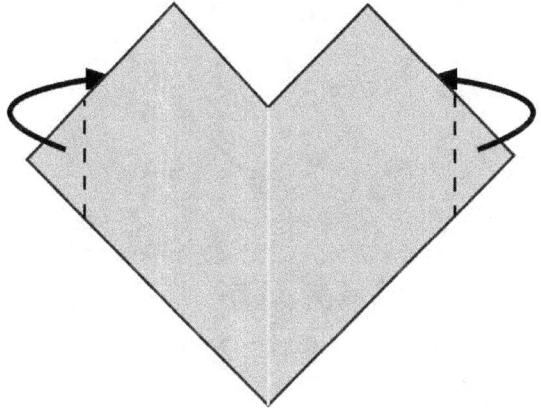

You're getting closer! Your paper should now look a little like the letter V.

Take the point of each side—again, on the left and the right—and fold just a little bit of it back. Do you see the arrows in the picture? They show you which direction to make the folds. In this step, for example, you need to fold the corners back and behind the heart.

Step 6

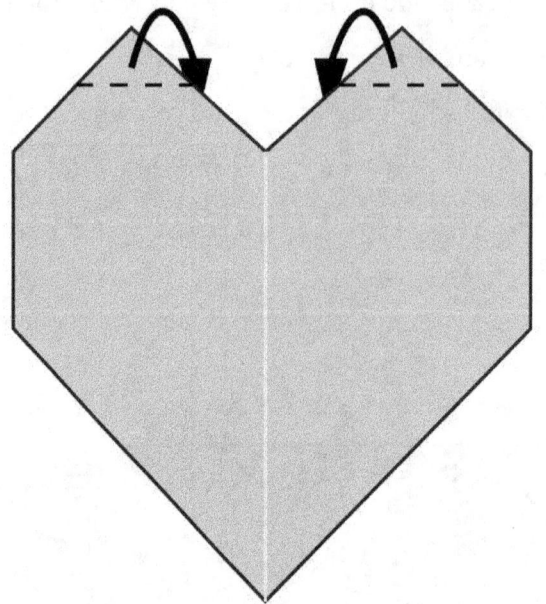

Now do the same thing to the two points at the top of the paper: fold them behind the heart.

Congratulations! You did it!

Give yourself a pat on the back. You just made your first origami figure, which is quite an accomplishment. And even better, you made a *heart*. Give it to someone special to you—then come right back and start the next chapter!

Chapter Five: A Cup

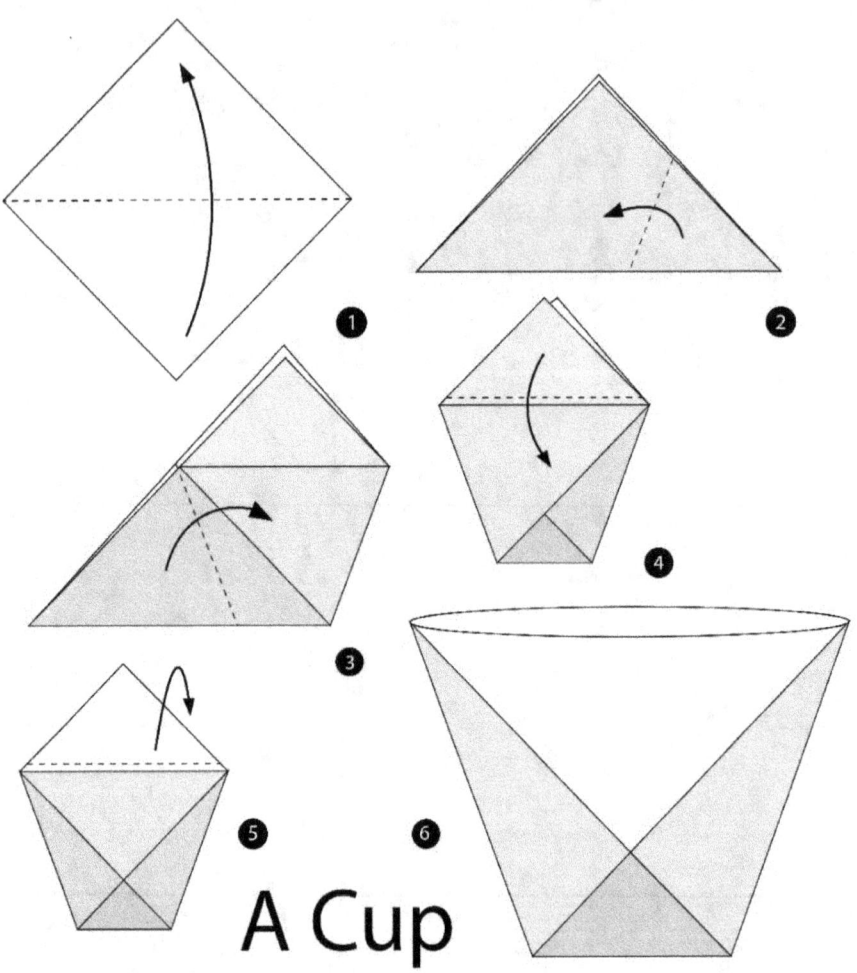

A heart is beautiful. But a cup?

Yes, an origami cup can be beautiful, especially with colorful paper. But even with plain paper, an origami cup can be interesting and fun to make. Just follow the simple instructions and in a matter of minutes, you'll be holding in your hand a cute little paper cup. I wouldn't put any water in it, though!

Step 1

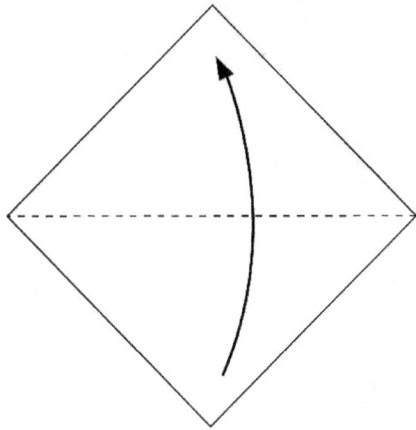

Just like you did with the origami heart, start with the square paper flat on the table. One of the corners should be pointing away from you.

By now you know what the dotted line means: it shows y   ere to make the fold. As you can see in the picture, you need to take the bottom corner (the one that's facing you) and bring it even with the top corner (the one that's facing away from you) and fold the paper in half right there.

Got it? Great! You just completed **Step 1**.

Step 2

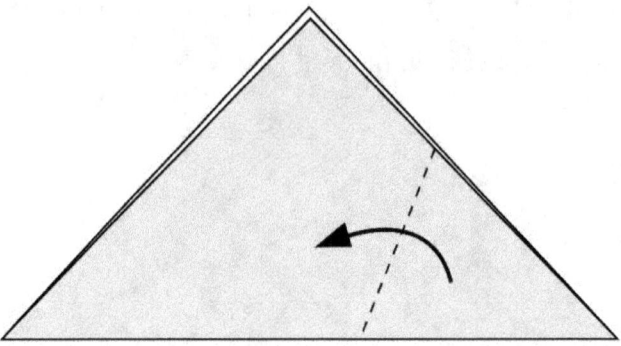

The paper should still be folded in half, with the points facing away from you.

Now take the right corner and fold it along the dotted line you see in the picture. The point of the right corner should now be touching the other side of the triangle, almost halfway down.

Step 3

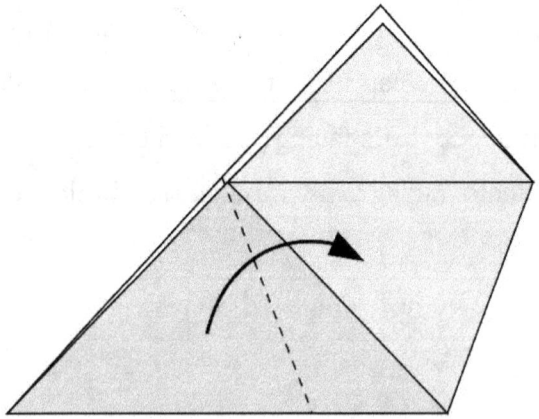

In **Step 3** you're going to do the same thing you did in **Step 2**, but from the other direction.

Take the left corner and fold it to the right along the dotted line you see in the picture. The point of the left corner should reach all the way to the right side. If this is confusing to you, don't worry, just look at the picture in **Step 4**. It will show you where the left corner should go, and what the figure should look like.

This is probably a good time to mention that if you make a mistake with your folds, it's okay. You're just beginning to learn an ancient art, so it's natural to make some mistakes along the way. If you ever fold something incorrectly, that's okay! Simply unfold it and try again. This is the time to learn and make mistakes. Very soon, you'll be making elaborate and artistic designs like people did 400 years ago in Japan.

Step 4

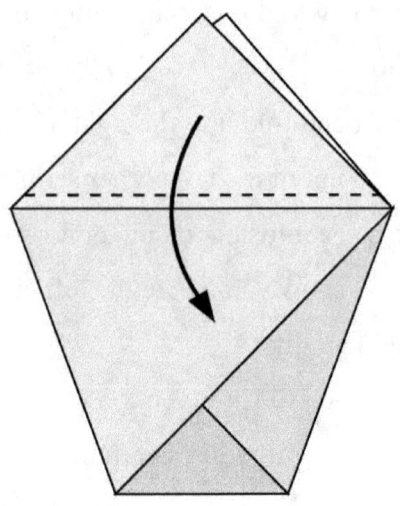

You now should have two flaps pointing up at the top of your cup. Take the flap that's closest to you and fold it downward along the dotted line you see in the picture. You'll notice that your earlier folds have made a little "pocket" along the inside of the cup. Tuck the flap closest to you into that little pocket.

Step 5

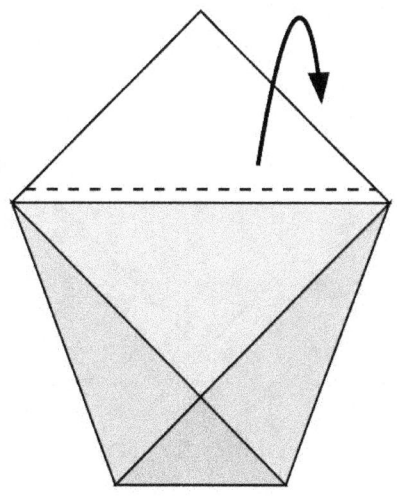

You now have one flap left.

Fold it downward like you see in the picture and tuck it into the cup. If you give the cup a gentle squeeze at its sides, it will open up and...

Boom! You're Done!

Congratulations, you've just completed your *second* origami. You'll be a pro in no time!

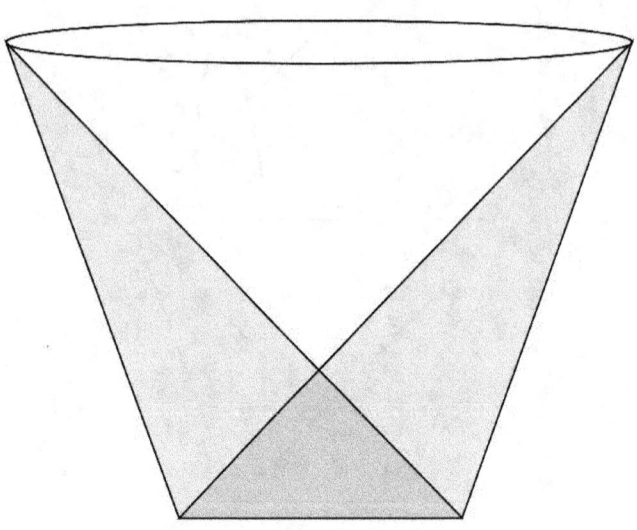

Chapter Six: A Letter

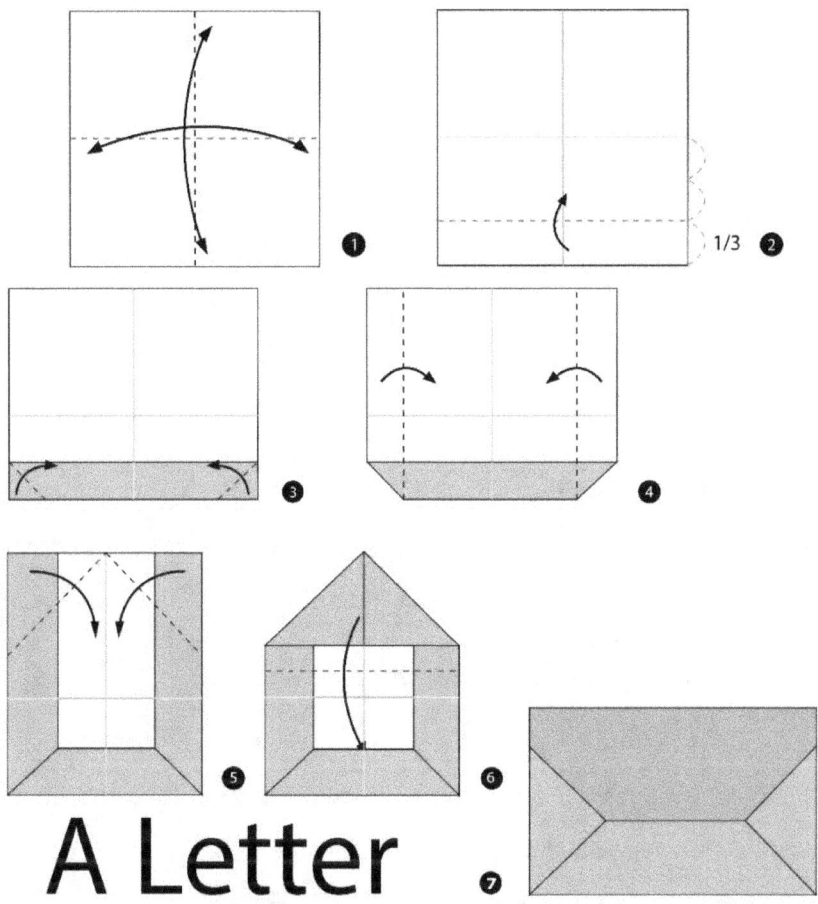

With all our technology—computers, cell phones, email—we've forgotten the joy that comes from receiving an actual handwritten letter. We text on our phones, we send many emails per day, and maybe we even have a video chat with a family member who is far away. These are all great things. But isn't it wonderful to know that someone took the time to sit down, grab a pen or pencil, and write you a *letter*? With this origami, you'll be able to give that joy to someone. And guess what? You won't even need to find an envelope to mail your letter—because, as you'll soon see, your letter *is* the envelope!

Step 1

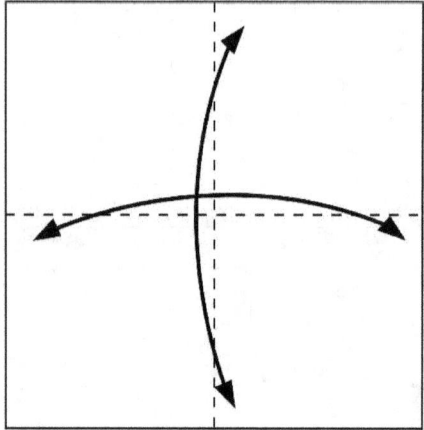

Lay your paper flat on the table in front of you. Make sure that none of the corners are pointing towards you or away from you. You want the paper to be positioned just like it is in the picture.

Now fold the paper along the dotted lines you see in the drawing. You will make two folds. The first will be up and down: take the top side of the square and fold it toward you until it is even with the bottom side. Now do the same thing again, only this time from side to side.

Step 2

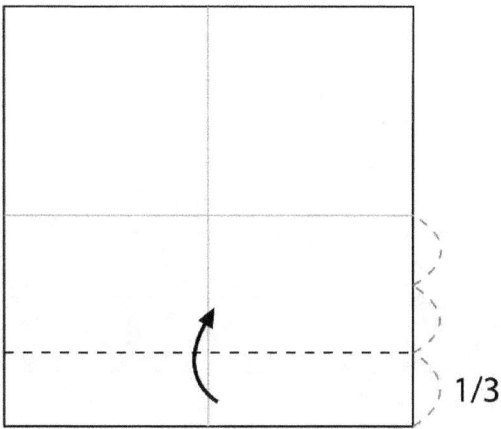

In this step, you're going to take the bottom edge of the square and fold it about 1/3 of the way toward the center. Imagine the bottom half of the square being divided into three pieces: now fold your paper about that much. If you look closely at the picture and fold where the dotted line is, you'll be just fine.

Again, you want to fold the bottom edge of the square 1/3 of the way toward the center.

Step 3

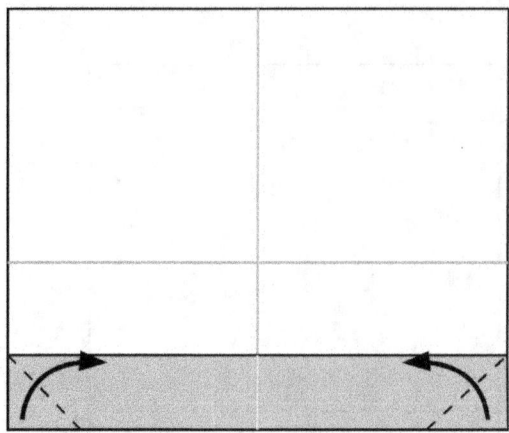

As you can see from the picture, you have already made your 1/3-fold. That's great. Now you need to fold the bottom corners inward toward the center. The dotted lines in the drawing show you where to fold. And remember, these need to be diagonal folds.

Step 4

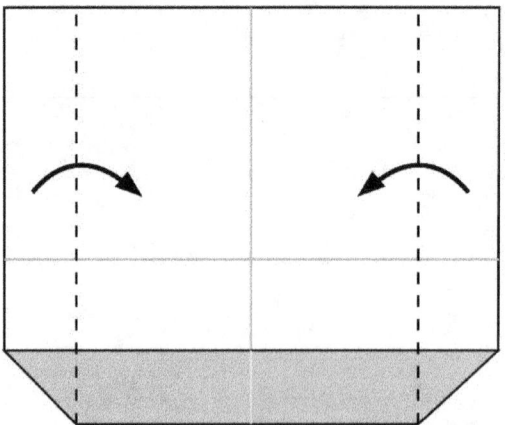

You're going to make two more folds. These will be moving from the outside in. Don't make the folds too close to the edges or too close to the center. If you base your folds on the dotted lines in the drawing, it'll be perfect. Start with the right side and then do the left. Be sure that your creases are nice and sharp. Those creases will be the sides of your envelope.

Step 5

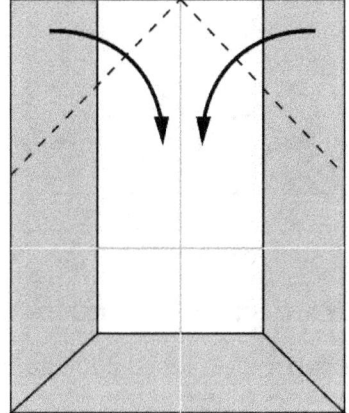

In this step you're going to take the two top corners and fold them diagonally towards the center. Study the picture and notice where the dotted lines are. Start with the top right corner and fold it along that line. Now do the same thing with the top left corner. If you make the folds correctly, then the edges of the two corners should be even with each other along the crease that runs down the center of the paper. If you need to back up and try again, that's perfectly okay. Take your time.

Step 6

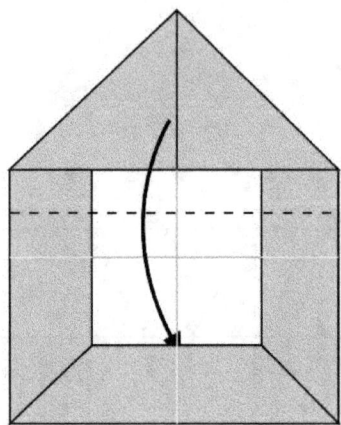

Now that your folds are correct and the top two corners have met in the center crease of the paper, you're going to fold down the top point of the paper. Notice where the dotted line is in the picture. Make your fold there.

Take another look at the picture. Do you notice how the tip of the arrow disappears behind the bottom flap of the paper? That's because when you make the fold and bring down the point, you need to take the point and tuck it behind that flap, just like the tip of the arrow.

Ready to Send! (Well, Almost…)

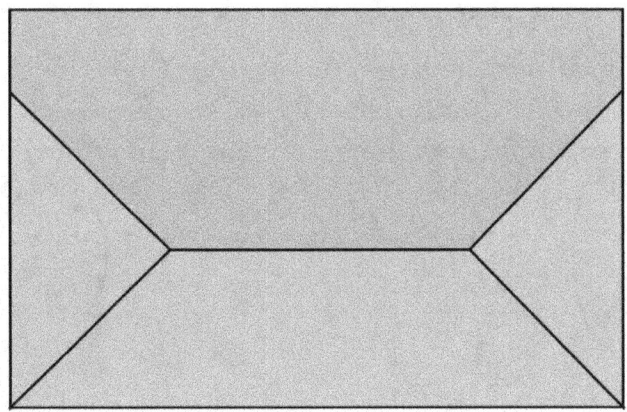

Once you tuck the top point behind the bottom flap, then you've "sealed" the envelope and you're ready to send it.

There's only one problem.

You didn't write a letter!

But that's okay. This time was just practice. Once you get comfortable making this type of origami, you'll be able to take a piece of paper, write a letter on it, and then fold it up just like you did this one. And whoever you write will be happy you did.

Chapter Seven: A Cicada

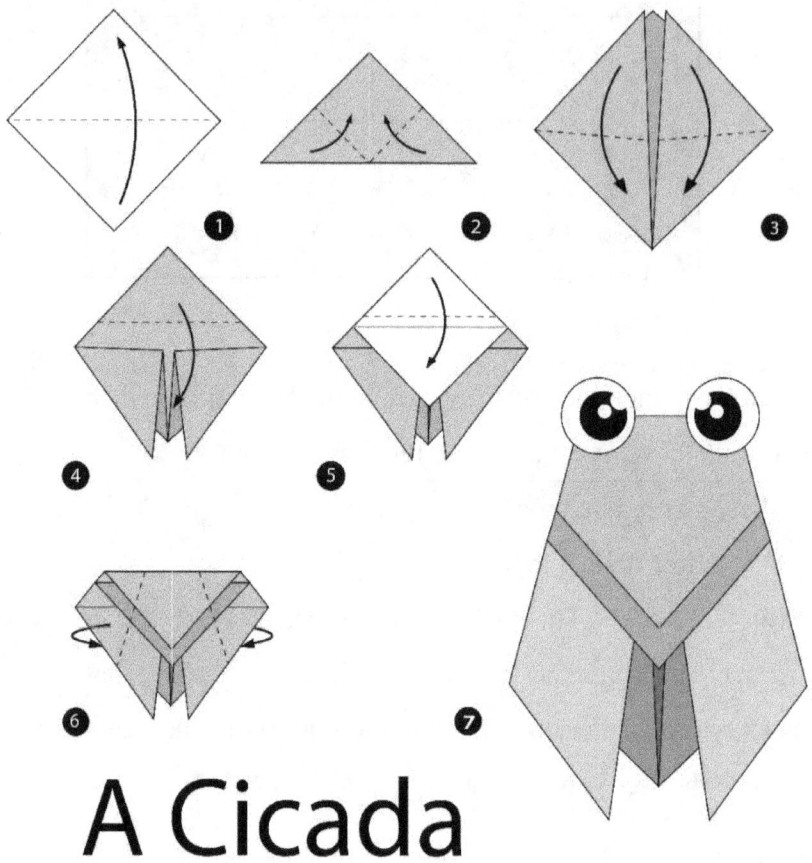

A Cicada

A cicada is a large flying insect that has a special and beloved place in Japanese culture. Do you know why? Because when they start buzzing—and they have a very loud buzz—it means that summer has arrived. So even though cicadas can be a little weird-looking, they're harmless and bring good news: Summer's here!

In Japan there are over 30 different kinds of cicada, and each has its own "song." Even though it just sounds like buzzing to most of us, the sounds made by cicadas are actually a form of communication. Some people like to listen to cicadas and try to hear the different songs.

And some people like to make cute little cicada origami!

Step 1

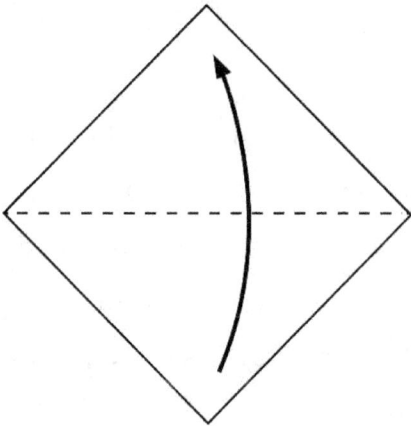

Place the square flat on the table as shown, with one corner pointing at you and one corner pointing away from you. You're going to fold the paper in half by taking the bottom corner (the one that's pointing at you) and lifting it toward the top corner (the one that's pointing away from you). Once you've made the fold, make sure you give it a good crease.

Step 2

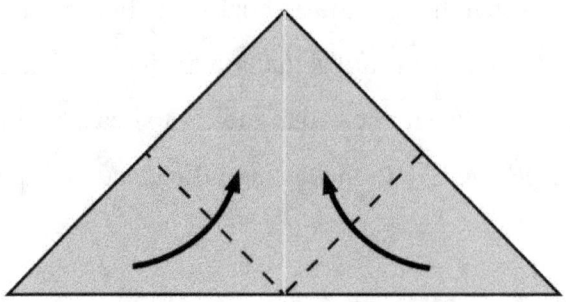

You should now have a triangle with a corner pointing away from you.

The next thing you're going to do is fold the two bottom corners toward the top. Take a look at the drawing. Notice where the dotted lines are. That's where you need to make your folds. Start with the right corner and fold it so that its edge is nearly even with the crease running down the center of the triangle (that's the solid gray line). Now do the exact same thing with the left corner.

Step 3

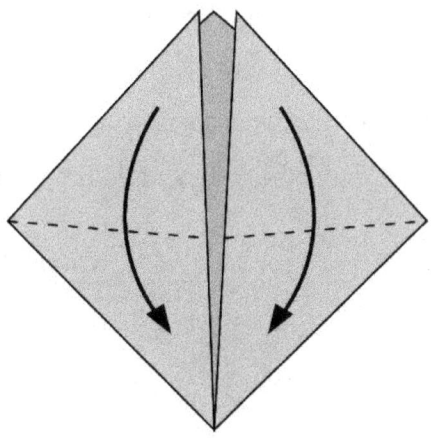

This is what your paper should look like now.

Next, you're going to take the two top flaps and fold down them along the dotted lines you see in the picture.

Step 4

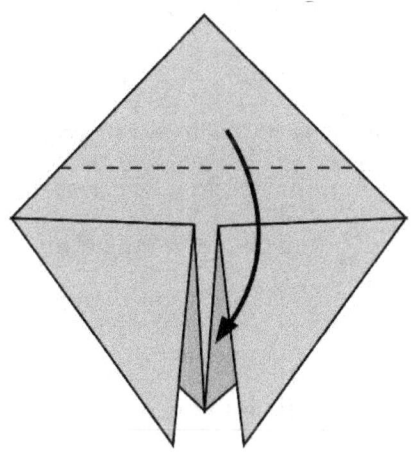

Once you've folded down the two flaps, you'll notice that there are two layers of paper pointing up. Take the layer closest to you and fold it down towards you, so that it covers parts of the two flaps you folded in **Step 3**. The dotted line in the drawing should help you know where to make the fold.

Step 5

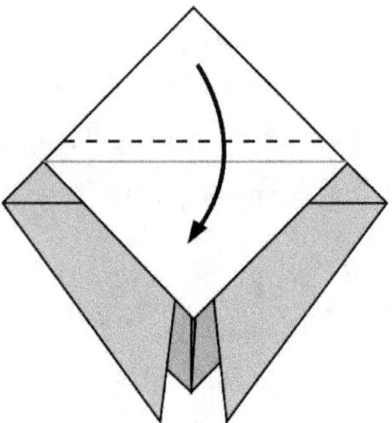

When you fold down the layer closest to you, you'll see that there's still one more layer. You will need to fold down that layer, too, but with an important difference. Notice that the dotted line in the drawing is just slightly above the previous fold. Don't make the mistake of simply folding both layers of paper over and creasing them together. You will want a slight difference in their fold lines, a slight space between the folds. If this is confusing, feel free to look ahead to the next step and study the picture. It'll give you a good idea of where the two folds should be.

Step 6

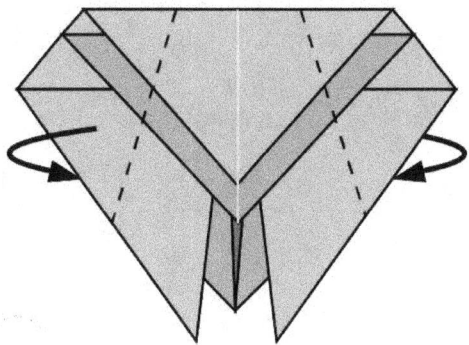

In this step, you're going to make two more folds. Starting with the right side of your paper, make a diagonal fold along the dotted lines. As you can see from the direction of the arrows in the picture, you will need to fold the paper *back* (behind the cicada) and make a good crease. Now move to the left side of the cicada and make a similar fold there. Again, you will be folding *behind* the cicada and making a firm crease.

Step 7

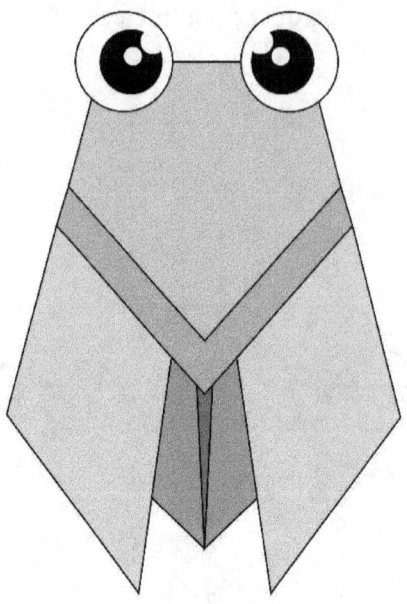

Take two plastic googly eyes and stick them on your cicada as shown in the drawing.

Ta-da!

You now have your very own pet cicada. Fortunately for you, *your* cicada doesn't do a lot of buzzing!

Chapter Eight: A Bird

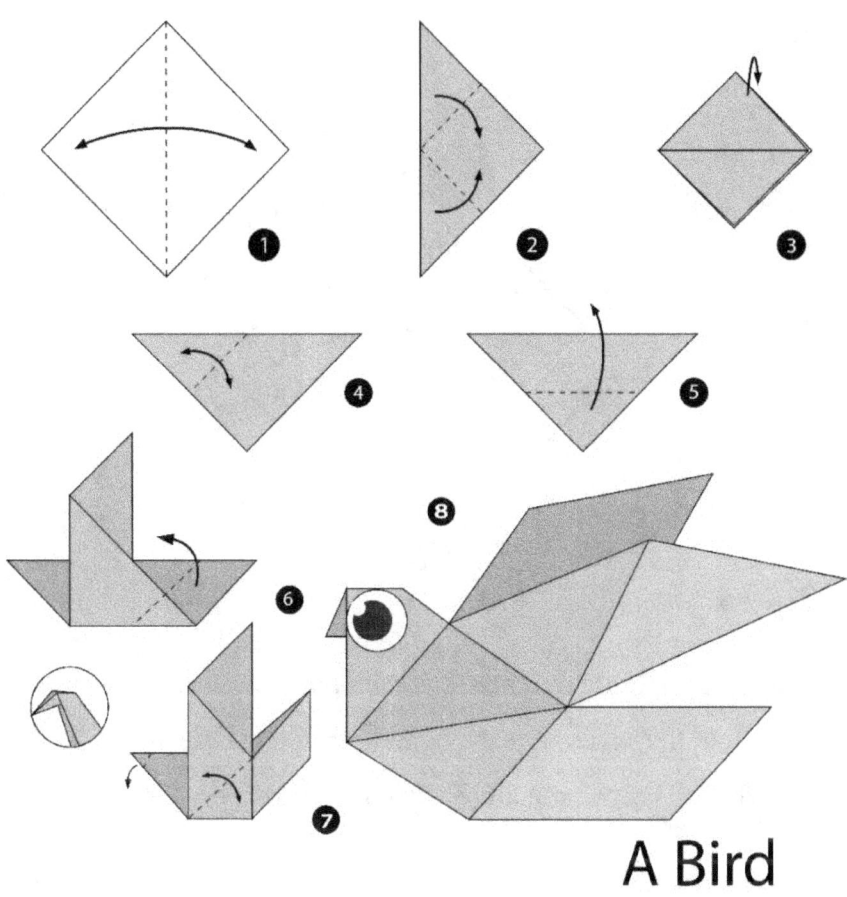

A Bird

Let's see: you made a heart, then you made a cup and a letter, and then you made an insect—now it's time to make an animal!

Animal patterns are very common in origami, and bird patterns are maybe the most popular. It's very appropriate, then, for you to have a bird as your first origami animal. You'll notice that this pattern is a little more difficult than any of the ones you've made so far. But you're learning fast and can do it!

Step 1

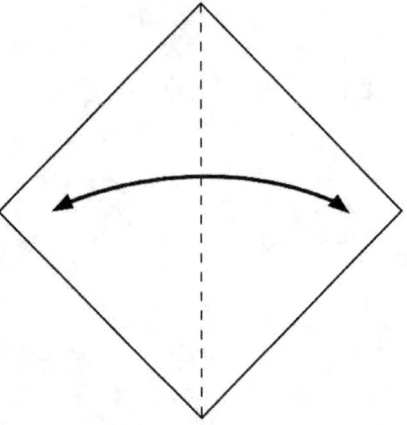

Place the paper flat on the table, with one corner facing away from you, then fold the square in half, right down the middle as shown in the picture. The left corner should be folded on top of the right corner.

Step 2

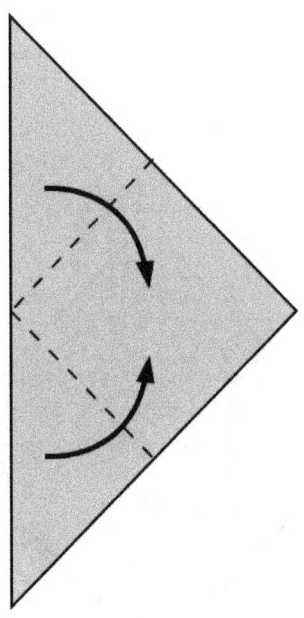

In front of you, the paper should now be a triangle pointing to the right.

Take the top corner (the one facing away from you) and fold it as shown in the picture. Once you make the fold, the point of the top corner should be lined up with the point of the corner to the right.

Now do the same thing with the bottom corner (the corner that's facing you).

When you have completed this step, both the top corner and the bottom corner should be lined up with the corner facing to the right.

Again, this may seem confusing at first. If you're unsure what things should look like after you've completed this step, simply look at the picture in **Step 3**. It will show you.

Step 3

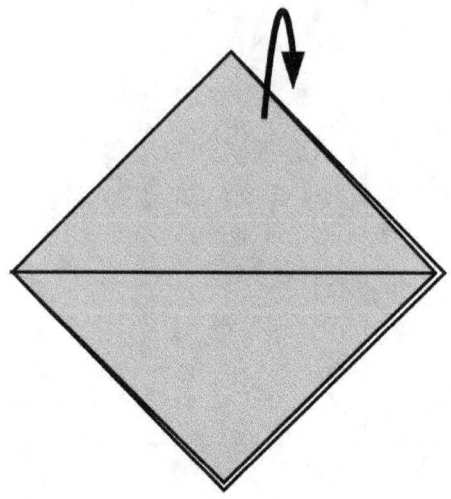

As you can tell from the arrow in the picture, you should now fold down the top half of the paper to the back. When you are done, you should have a triangle with a corner pointing towards you on the table.

Step 4

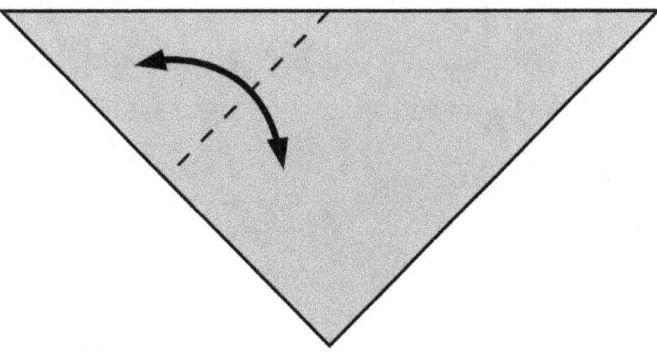

Take the left corner and fold it along the dotted line as in the picture.

Now unfold it.

Step 5

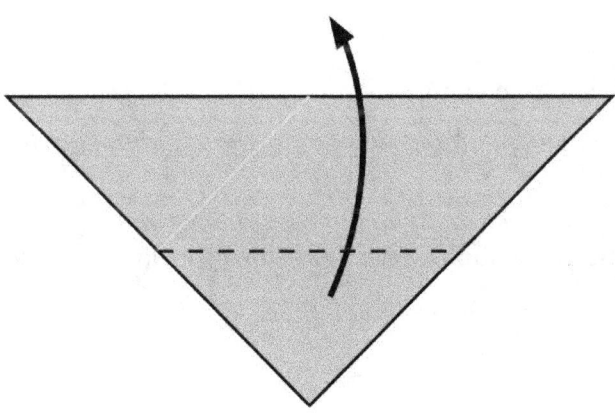

Do you see the solid gray line in the picture? Do you remember what it means? That's right: it's the crease you made in the previous step. Now fold the bottom corner up along the dotted line.

Step 6

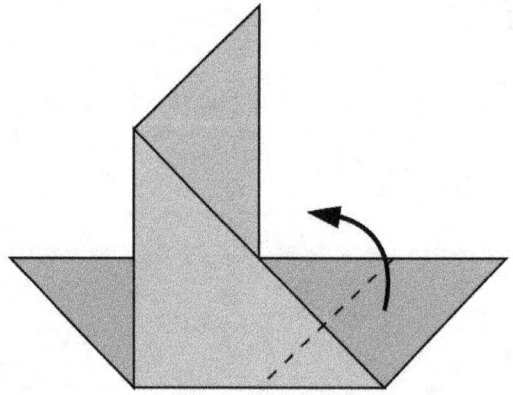

Let's create some wings!

This fold may require a couple of tries to get right, but once you do, you'll have it forever.

Open the paper slightly and fold along the dotted line you see in the picture.

Step 7

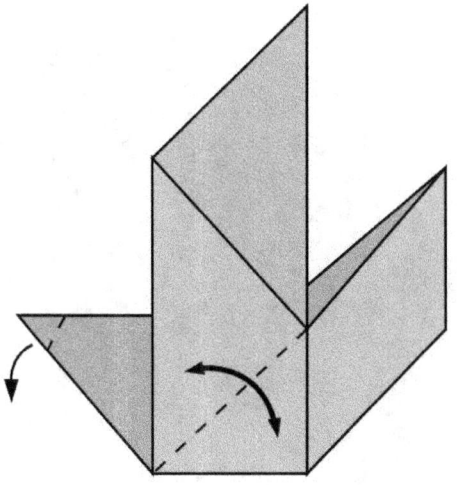

This step actually has two folds.

To make the first one, look at the double-sided arrow. A double-sided arrow means that you'll make a fold in both directions along the dotted line.

The second fold is much simpler: just follow the single-sided arrow and fold the tip of that little corner back. Congratulations! You just make a bird beak!

Step 8

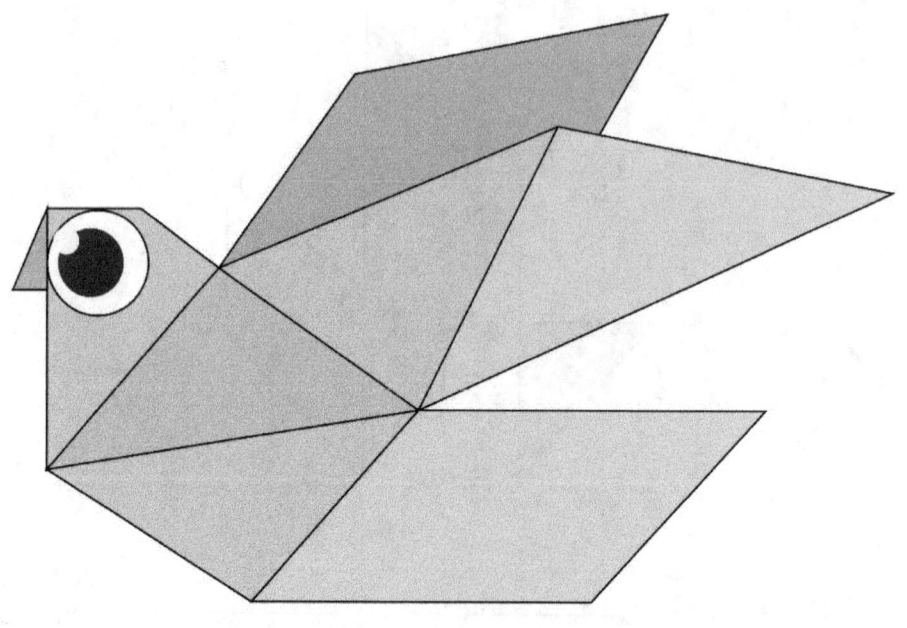

Although you don't *have* to do anything more, it's always fun to add an eye. You can either draw an eye with a magic marker, or you can stick on a googly eye from the craft supply store.

Either way, you're done! Great job!

Chapter Nine: A Little Boat

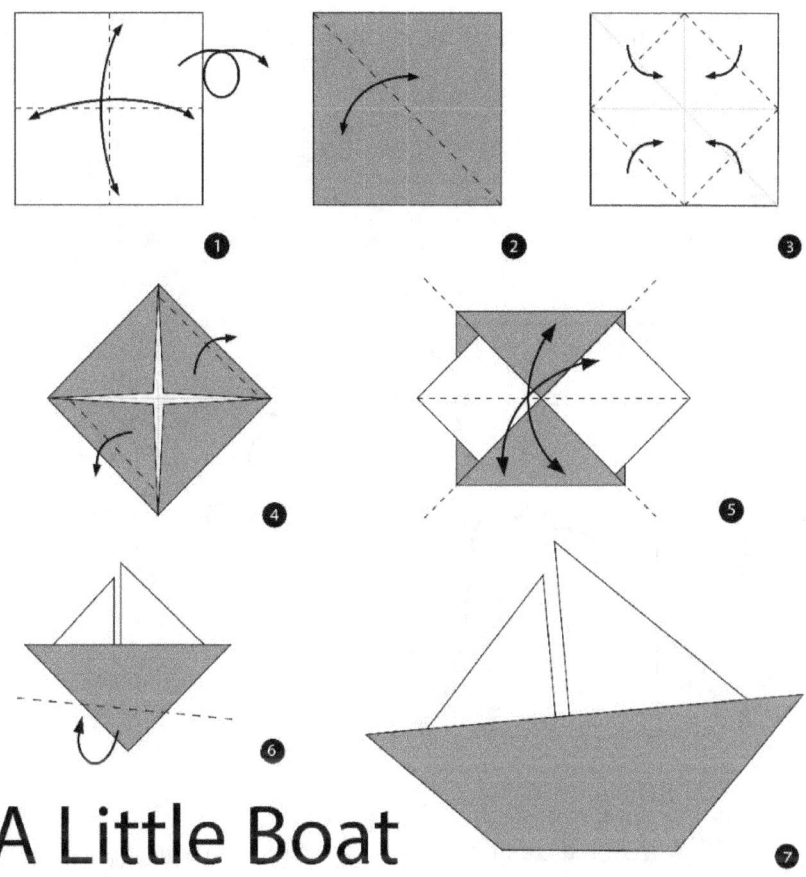

Japan is an island. It is surrounded by water on all sides. In the years before airplanes were invented, the Japanese had to travel by boat if they wanted to visit China, Korea, or even the United States. The Japanese have a long history of making boats, which is why boats are very popular origami figures.

Although a big boat made out of paper probably wouldn't make it across the ocean, an *origami* boat made out of paper just might make it across a bathtub or sink filled with water!

This pattern is not too difficult, but it still offers the opportunity to learn some new folds. Here we go....

Step 1

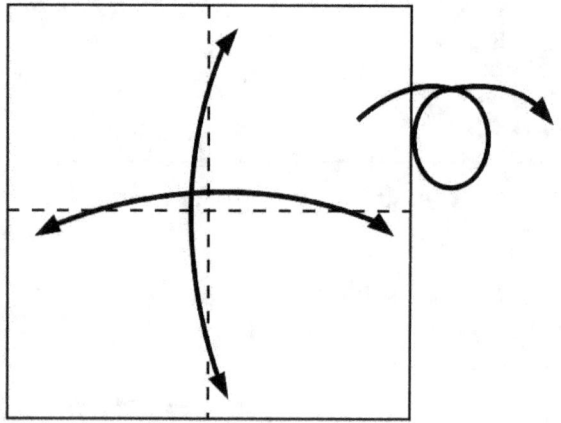

You'll notice that this time there are no corners facing you (or facing away from you). Place the square flat as shown, then fold it in half left to right and up and down.

Remember the looping arrow symbol? That means you need to turn the square over and make the same two folds on the other side of the paper.

Step 2

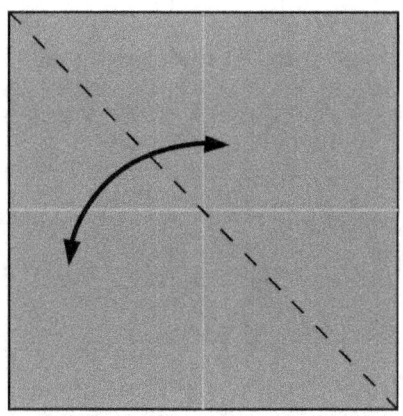

With the paper now face-down on the table, fold it in half diagonally as shown in the picture, then unfold it.

Step 3

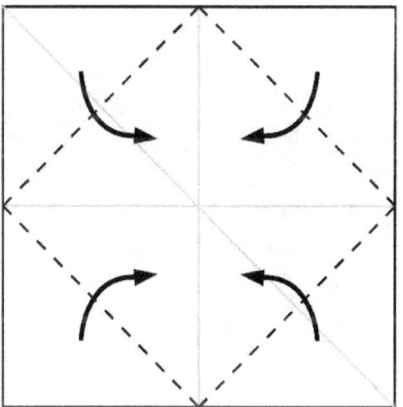

This step has four folds, so look at the picture carefully.

Don't panic, it's a lot simpler than it looks.

Notice the solid gray lines. At this point, you should have three creases in your paper: up and down, side to side, and diagonally.

The first thing you're going to do is turn the paper over again and return it to its original position.

The next thing you're going to do is take each corner and fold it as shown, so that each corner touches the very center of the square.

That's a lot of folding for one step, so if this is confusing to you in any way, don't hesitate to look ahead at the picture in **Step 4**; it should make everything clear.

Step 4

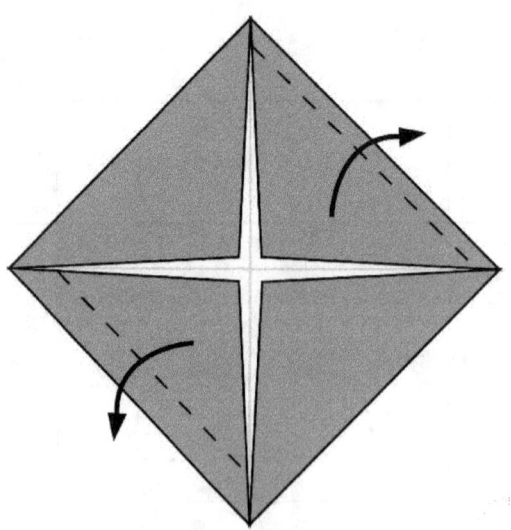

Take a good look at the dotted lines in the picture. You'll notice that they're a little different from each other. The one at the top is closer to the side than the one at the bottom. This will be important later, so make sure you notice it now and make your folds correctly.

Let's start with the top right corner. Take the corner and fold it back from the center in the direction of the arrow. Make sure that the fold is close to its side, as shown in the picture.

Now let's move to the bottom left corner. Take that corner and fold it back from the center in the direction of the arrow. Make sure that this fold is a little farther away from its side, as shown in the picture. This will be important in just a moment.

Step 5

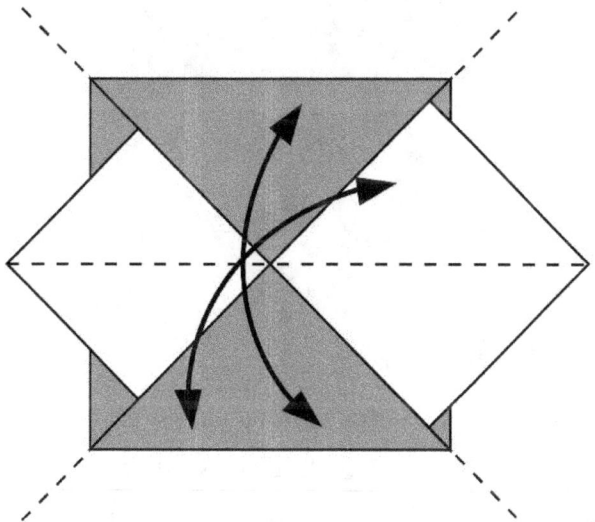

This step will fold the square in half three ways.

The first fold will be up and down, as shown by the dotted lines. The second fold and third folds, also shown by the dotted lines, will be diagonal. Take the bottom left corner and fold it up to the top right corner. For the third fold, again follow the dotted lines and fold the bottom right corner up to the top left corner.

Step 6

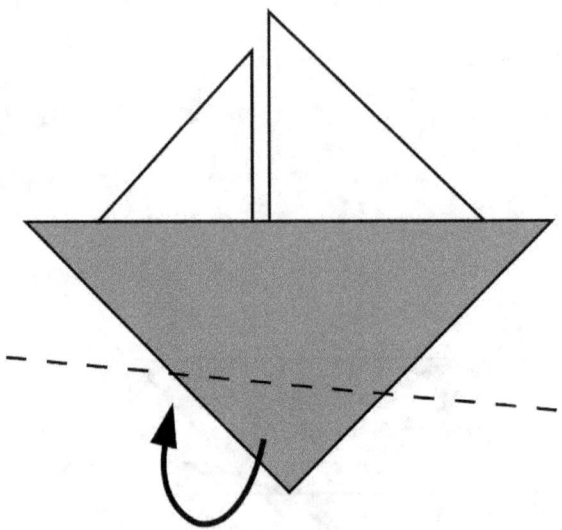

You now only have one more fold.

Take the bottom point (which is facing you) and fold it back behind the boat. Make sure you make the fold at a slight angle as shown in the picture. Although you don't *have* to do it at an angle, it makes the boat look cuter and somehow more realistic.

Ahoy! You Did It!

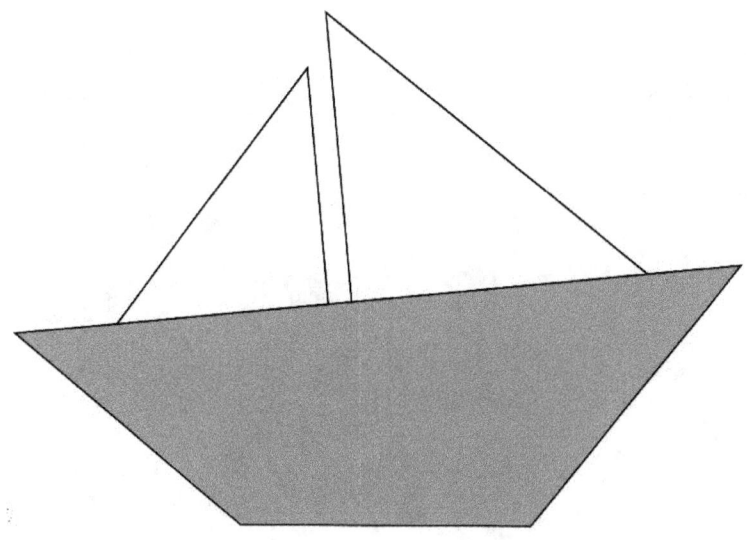

This little boat can sit proudly on your desk, or, if you're adventurous, it can float in your tub or sink.

Good job!

Chapter Ten: A Headfish

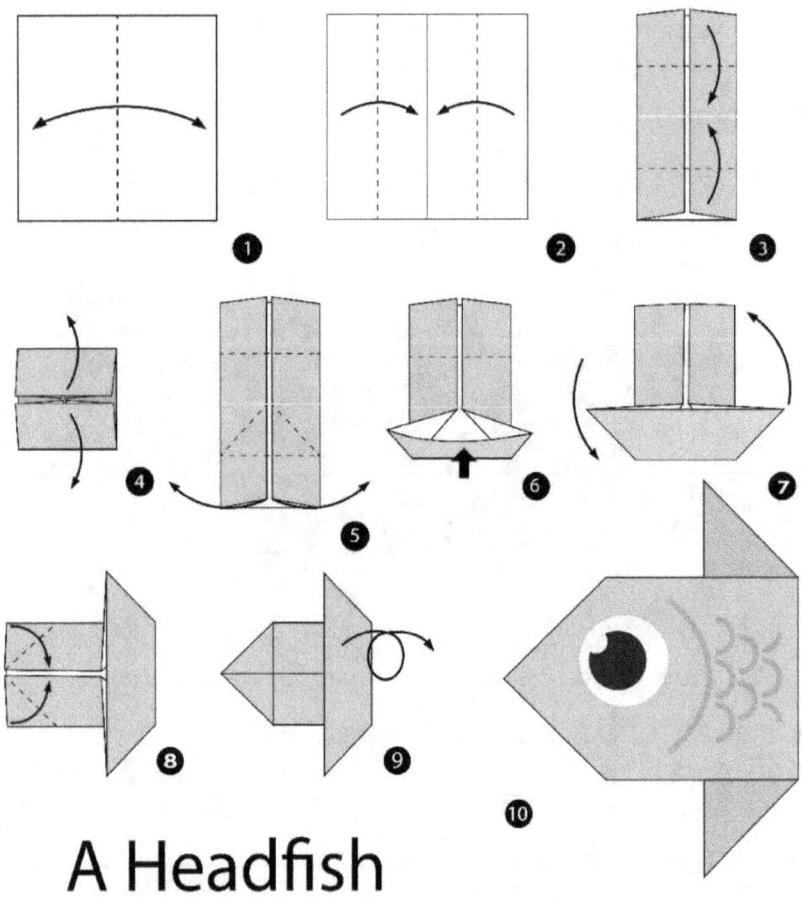

A Headfish

Well, now that you have a boat, it's time to go fishing!

The seas that surround Japan are full of fish, and the Japanese have a great love of fishing and of eating seafood. A headfish is an unusual creature that gets its name from its weird shape: it's body appears to be mostly head. They're actually a type of sunfish and are considered in Japan a real treat.

Luckily for us, the headfish's odd shape makes it an easy origami to learn. Plus, it will allow you to use your magic markers and plastic googly eyes.

Step 1

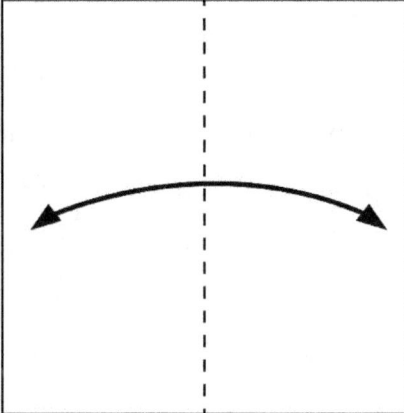

Place the paper flat on the table as in the picture. Fold it in half.

Step 2

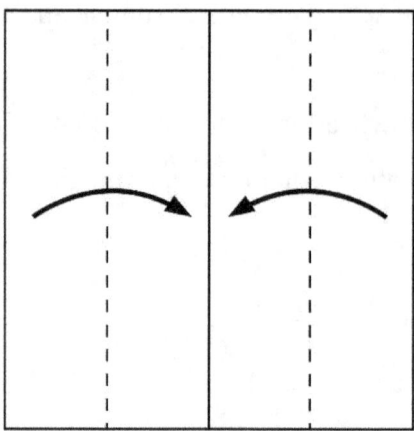

Unfold the paper and smooth it flat in the table again. You're now going to make two new folds, one from the right side and one from the left side. Basically, you're going to fold each half *in half*. Got that? Just remember to fold each side toward the center crease.

Step 3

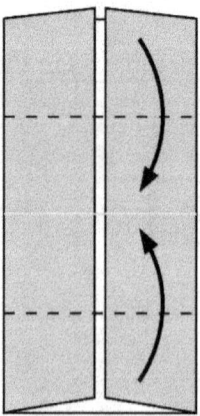

You're again going to make two folds in this step. Starting at the bottom, fold the bottom half of the paper upward, until the bottom side reaches the middle. Do you see that solid white line across the middle of the picture? That's the imaginary middle of the paper. Bring the bottom side of your paper upward and make it even with that.

Now do the same thing, only this time from the top.

Step 4

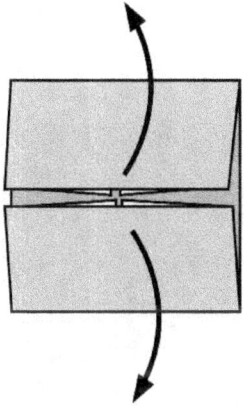

This step is very simple: just unfold the top and bottom so that the paper looks just like it did at the start of **Step 3**.

Step 5

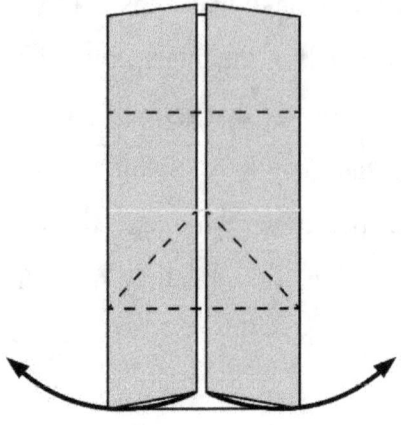

Make folds along the diagonal dotted lines, as you see in the picture.

Step 6

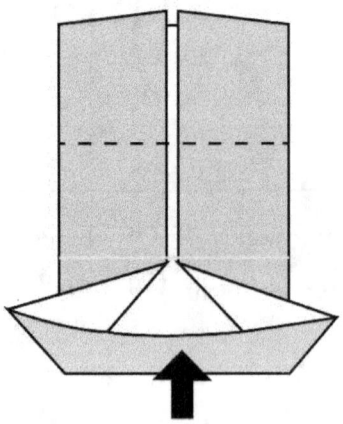

This next move looks a little hard, but once you start doing it, you'll see that it's actually very easy. Just pull the very bottom side down and out, then fold it back up, pressing against the diagonal creases you just made in **Step 5**.

Step 7

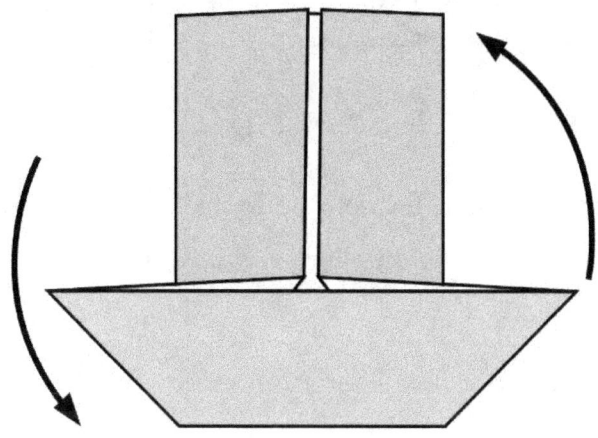

This is what your paper should look like now. The next thing to do is turn it sideways to the left.

Step 8

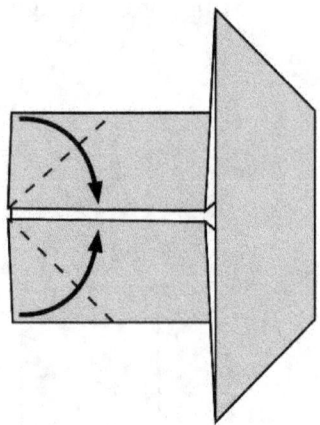

Now make fold along the dotted diagonal lines, like you see in the picture. Just be sure to fold the paper *toward* you.

Step 9

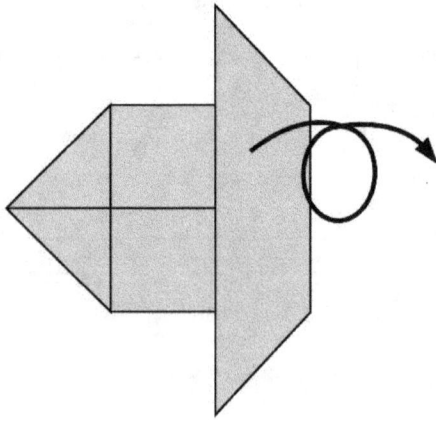

This is what your paper should look like now. Do you see the looping arrow? That means to turn the paper over.

Step 10

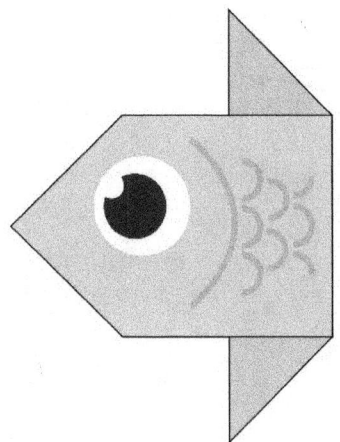

Almost there…

Grab a magic marker and draw some scales and a gill. Then take one of the plastic googly eyes you got at the craft store and stick it on your headfish.

You're done!

Chapter Eleven: A Peacock

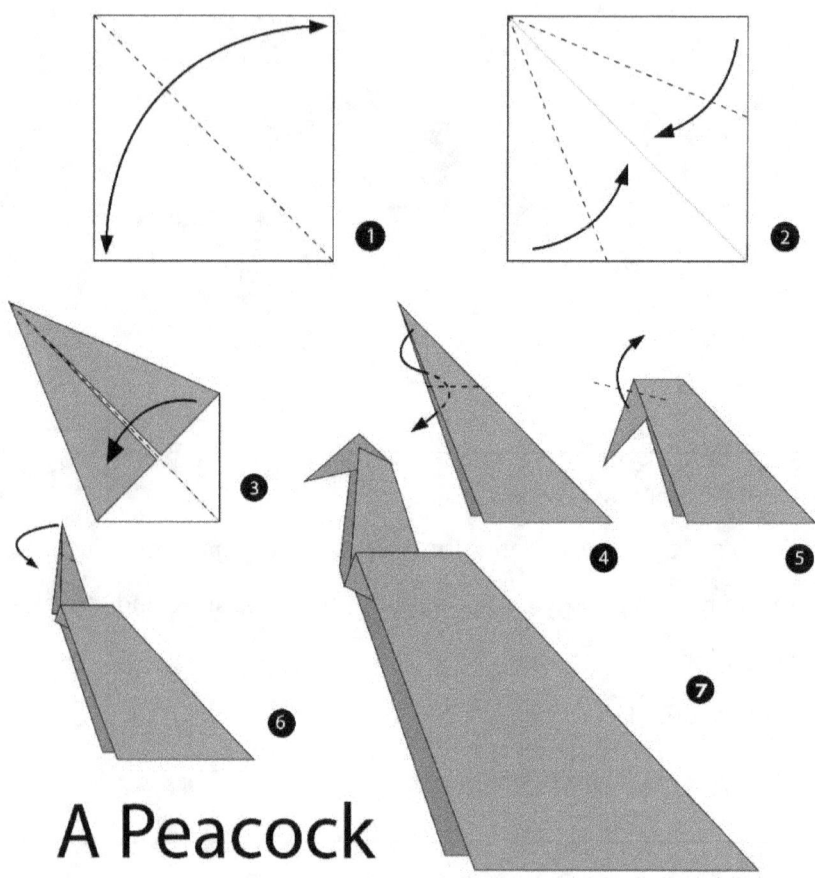

Back in Chapter Six you made a bird. What kind of bird was it? Whatever kind of bird you wanted it to be.

This time, though, you're going to make a specific kind of bird. This time, you're going to make a peacock.

The peacock is a symbol of compassion and kind-heartedness, and it is believed to have the power to defeat poison and even make it rain. In Japanese culture, it is associated with good health. The peacock is a good symbol and a good origami to make.

Step 1

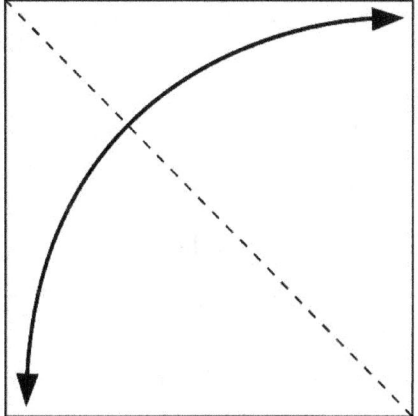

Place the square flat on the table as shown and fold it in half diagonally. Bring the bottom left corner up to the top right corner, make a crease, then unfold the paper.

Step 2

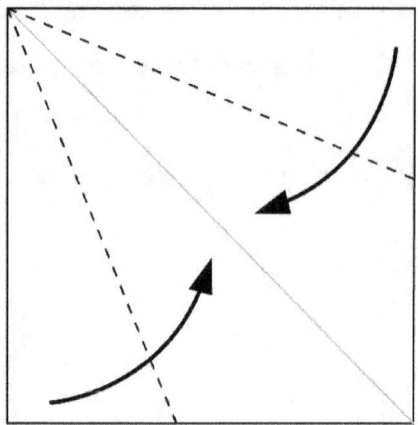

This next fold will be familiar to anyone who's ever made a paper airplane. Fold the top right corner down along the dotted line, so that the top of the square is even with the center crease.

Now do the same thing with the bottom left corner.

Step 3

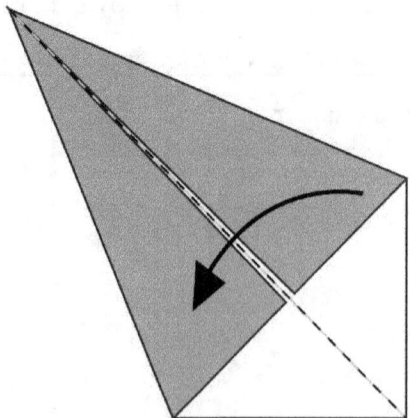

Now fold the figure in half, as shown. It kind of looks like you're about to make a paper airplane, but you're not.

Step 4

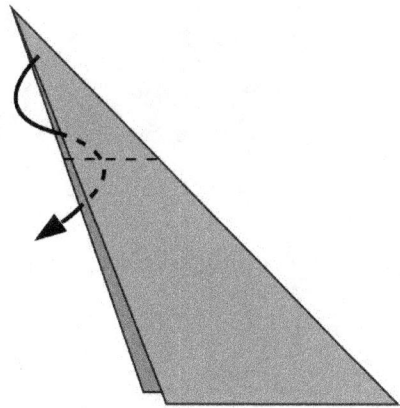

This next move is kind of neat.

Fold the paper near the top, as shown by the dotted lines. Fold the paper both ways.

Then, here comes the neat part: you're going to take that top point and follow the arrow down. In other words, you're going to "turn the paper inside out," so that the figure will look like the picture in **Step 5** below.

Step 5

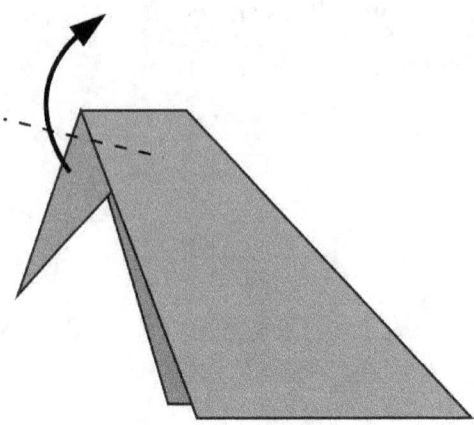

Now reverse what you just did and bring the point back up—but make a fold along the dotted lines as you do it.

Step 6

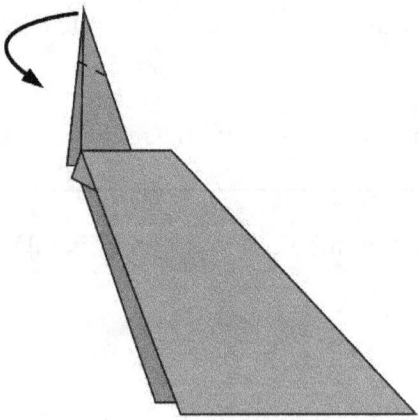

The only thing left for you to do now is make the beak. You do this by making a fold along the dotted lines, then by pushing the paper inside the figure and flattening it along the creases you've already made. By the way, this type of origami fold is called an inside reverse fold.

Success!

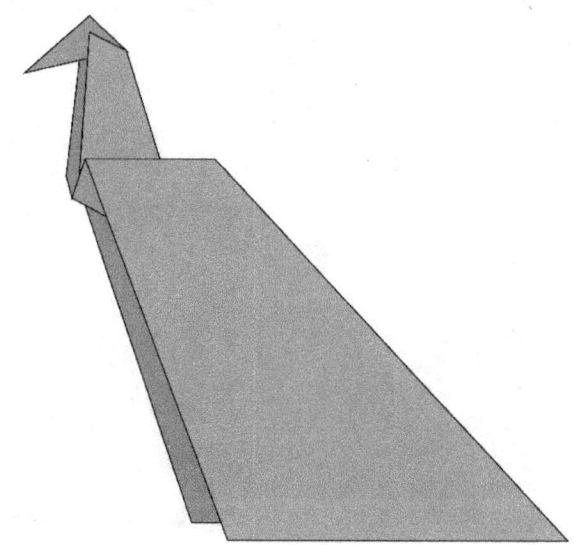

You've completed your second bird, this one a majestic peacock. You're on a roll!

Chapter Twelve: A Fox Face

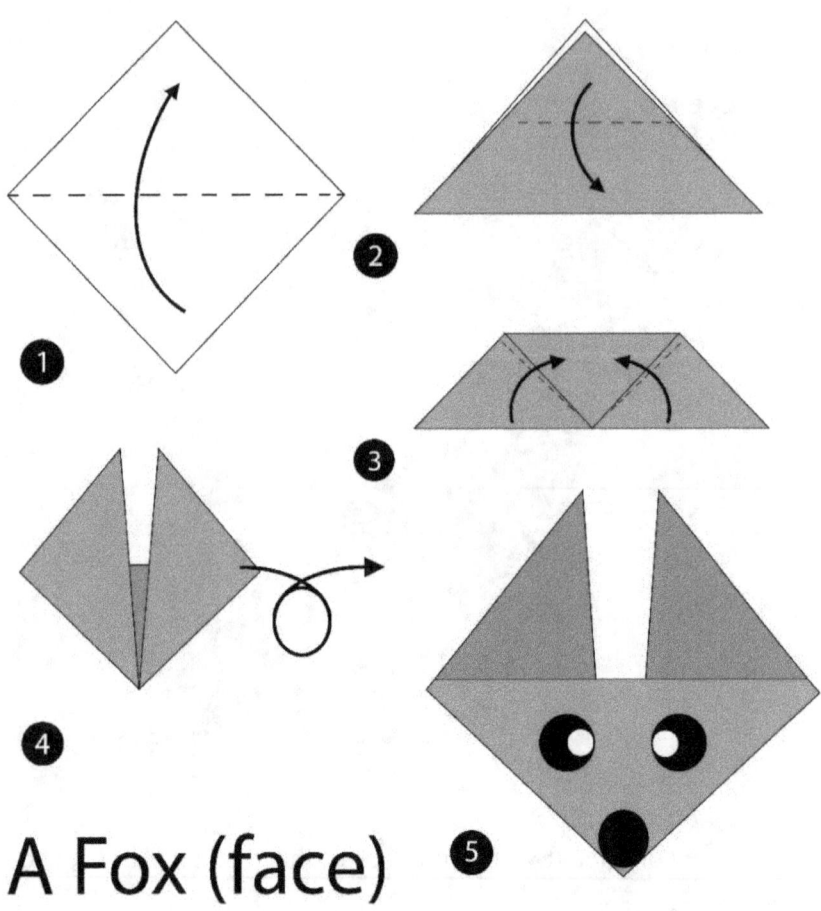

What do you say we take a little break and relax?

That last pattern was a kind of complex, so maybe you'd like to catch your breath and enjoy an easy one.

Plus, this pattern will give you an excuse to use some more googly eyes.

But first, did you know that the Japanese word for fox is *kitsune*? Here it is:

In ancient Japan, foxes and humans lived closely together, and this closeness generated legends about the creatures. Foxes were seen as somehow supernatural and were believed to be the messengers of spirits and gods. In many Japanese folktales, foxes have the ability to change into humans—sometimes to trick humans, sometimes to help them.

Now that you know a little about the *kitsune*, or fox, it's time to make one!

Step 1

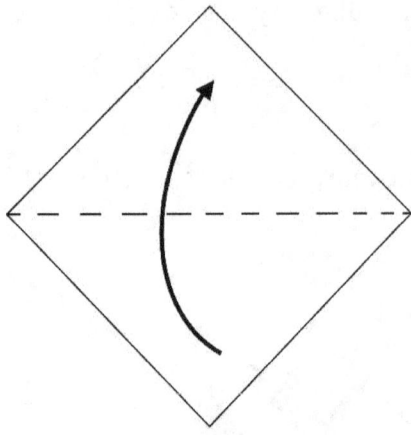

Position the paper so that one of the squares is facing away from you. Fold it in half along the dotted line.

Step 2

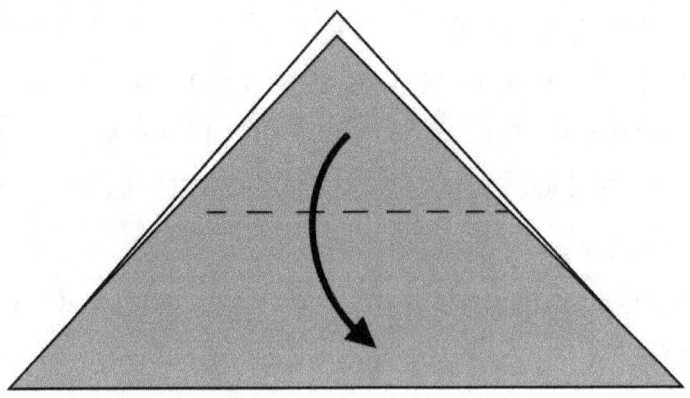

Take the two corners pointing up and fold them (both of them, not just one of them) down towards you. The points should touch the bottom of the paper, as shown in **Step 3**.

Step 3

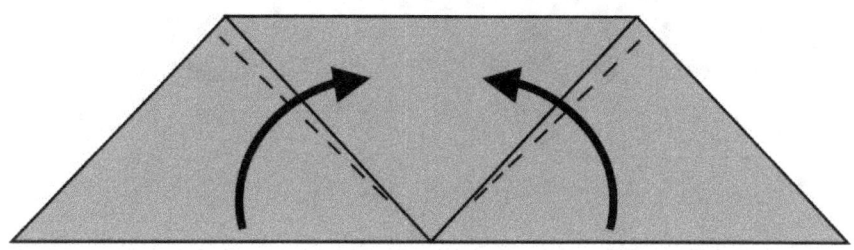

Now you're going to make some fox ears.

Take each of the corners and fold them up, following the arrows.

Step 4

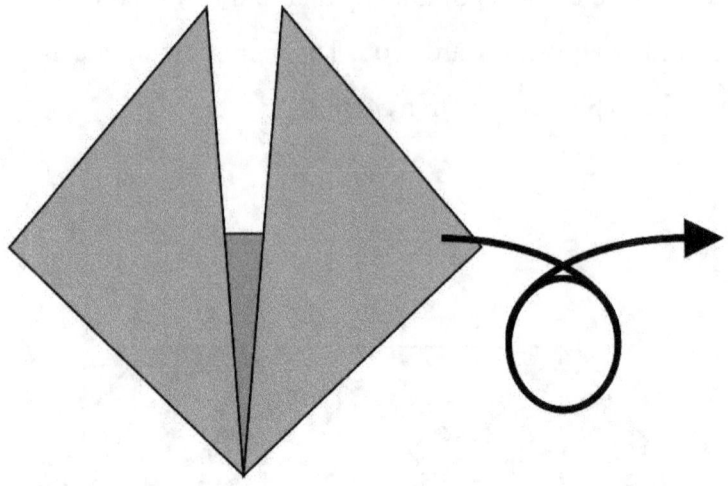

Are you starting to see it?

You know what that looping arrow means.

Turn the whole thing over.

Step 5

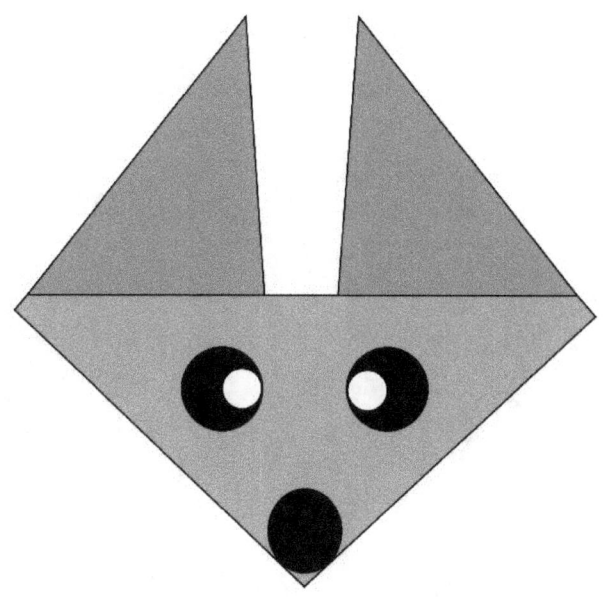

It's googly eye time!

Take your magic marker and fill in a round little nose for your fox. Then stick some googly eyes on it and you're done!

Chapter Thirteen: A Cat

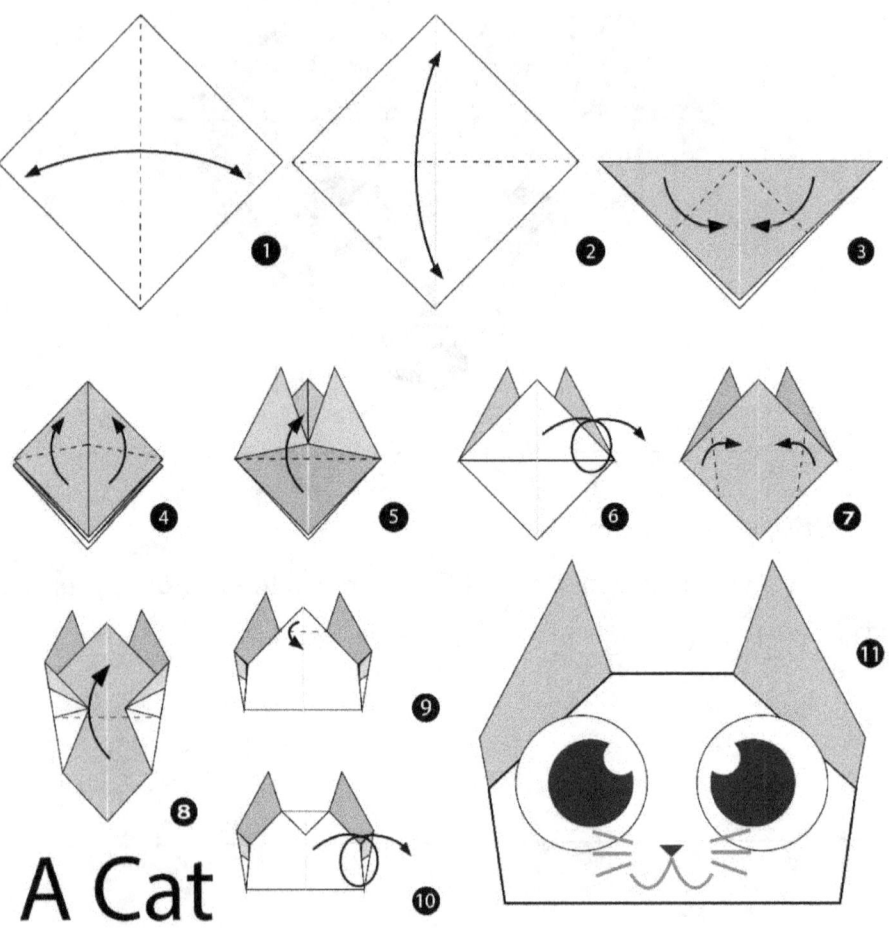

Have you ever seen someone with a headfish for a pet? Me neither. But you probably *have* seen lots of people with *cats* for pets. Cats are among the most popular animals on the planet, so it's fitting that they should be popular among origami artists.

In Japan, cats are believed to bring good luck and other positive results. There is a popular Japanese cat figurine called "beckoning cat" that is often given as a gift to bring blessings. The figurine usually has a cat with its paw raised, as if waving hello or calling you over. According to Japanese legend, a landlord witnessed a cat waving a paw at him. Intrigued, he came close to the cat. Suddenly a lightning bolt struck the exact spot where he had been previously standing. The landlord believed that his good fortune was because of the cat's actions. Ever since then, the beckoning cat has been a symbol of good luck. These little figurines are mostly found at the entrances of shops, restaurants, and other businesses.

This pattern will be a little challenging, so pay close attention to the pictures.

Step 1

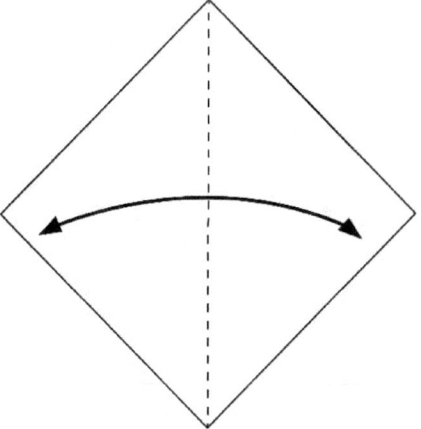

As you so often do, you'll start with the paper flat on the table with a corner facing away from you. Fold the paper in half down the middle, from side to side.

Step 2

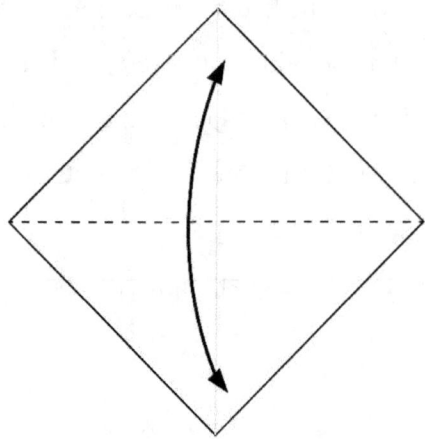

Now fold the square again, this time up and down. Bring the top corner and place it on top of the bottom corner, so that you have a triangle with a point facing towards you.

Step 3

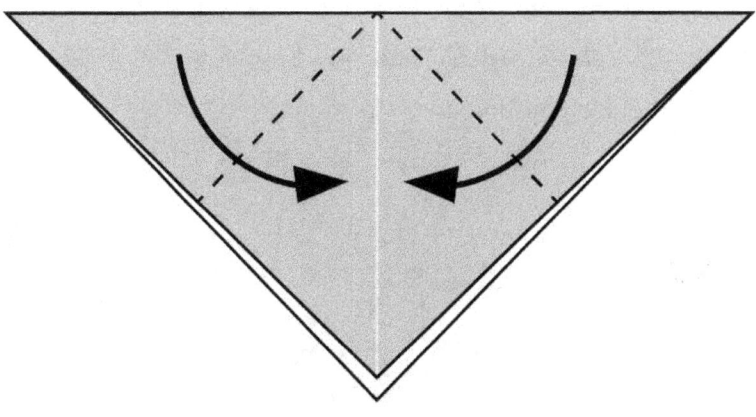

Now make folds along the diagonal dotted lines in the picture. Always remember to bend your folds in the direction of the arrows.

Step 4

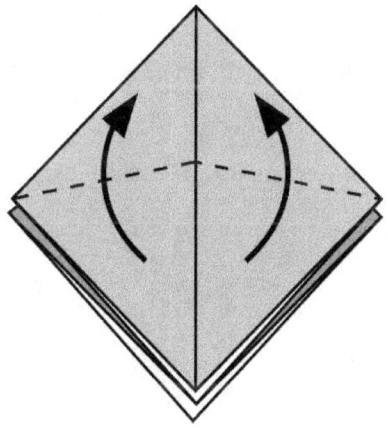

You should have two small flaps pointing toward you now. They're on top. Pull the two flaps up and fold them along the dotted lines so that they're pointing away from you.

Step 5

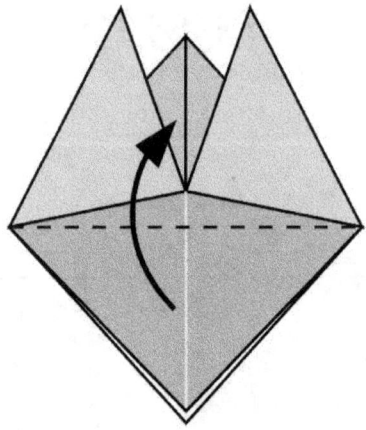

When you fold those two smaller flaps up, you reveal a larger flap that's pointing toward you. Fold *that* flap up and crease it along the dotted line.

Step 6

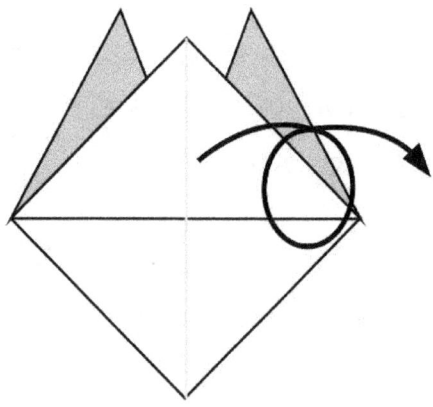

This is what your paper should look like at this point. Now take the whole pattern and turn it over.

Step 7

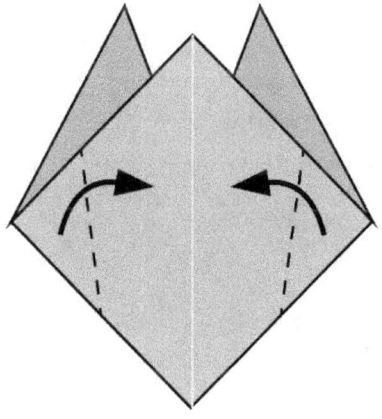

Take each side and fold the points inward, toward the center crease (the solid gray line you see in the picture). But make sure the points don't actually *touch* the center crease. Look at the drawing in **Step 8** if you're unsure how far to fold your points.

Step 8

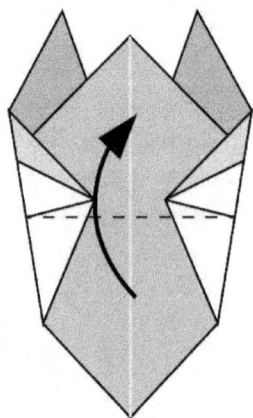

Now you're going to fold the entire pattern in half. Take the bottom point (which is pointing toward you) and fold it up so that it is even with the top point (which is facing away from you).

Step 9

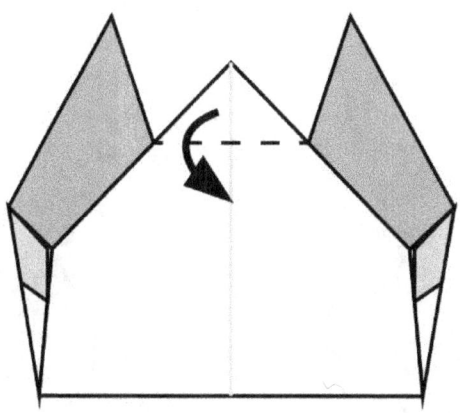

Take the back point and fold it down (towards you) along the dotted line you see in the drawing.

Step 10

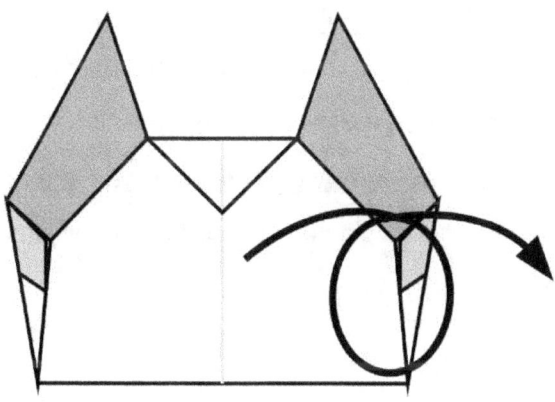

Now flip the entire pattern over.

Step 11

Take a black or brown magic marker and draw some whiskers on your cat face. Remember that cat's noses are shaped like upside-down triangles. When you take your marker and draw a nose for your cat, make it look like the one in the picture above.

Then take two plastic googly eyes and stick them on the paper. Congratulations! You've made yourself a cute origami cat!

Chapter Fourteen: A Tulip

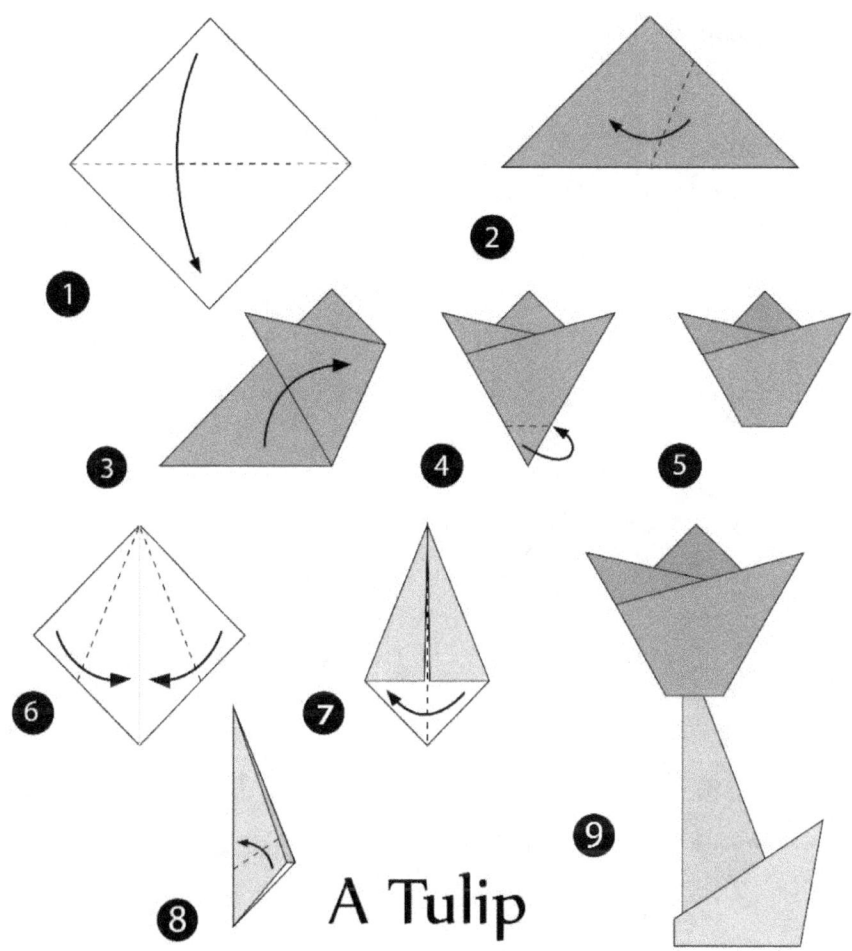

In Japan, tulips bloom in late April and early May, and make the springtime bright and colorful. They are very popular flowers in Japan. In fact, in Tokyo (which, if you'll remember from Chapter One, used to be called Edo), there is a big tulip festival every year that attracts thousands of people.

This is a simple pattern, but it requires something new: a second piece of paper.

Step 1

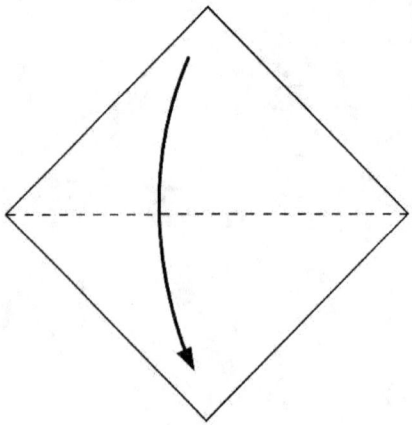

Place the paper so that one of the corners is facing away from you. Fold the paper in half, bringing the bottom to the top.

Step 2

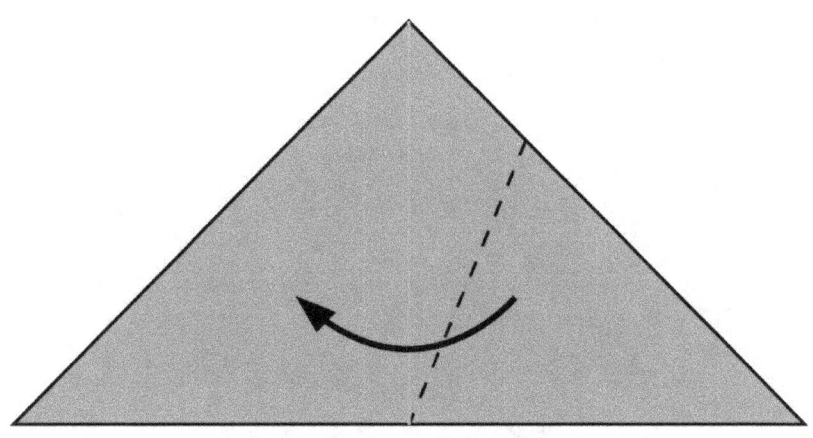

Make a fold along the dotted line shown in the drawing above. This is similar to the fold you made earlier with the cup.

Step 3

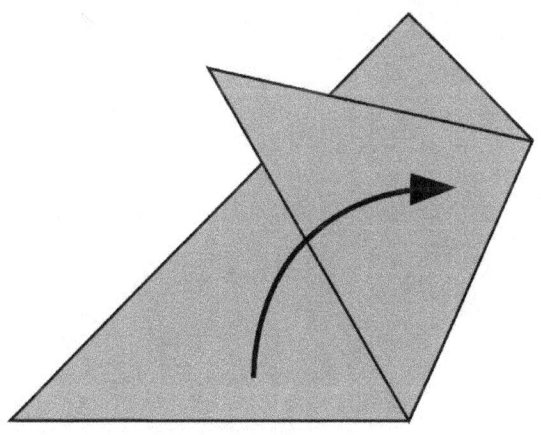

Once you have folded the right corner over, do the same thing with the left corner, folding in the direction of the arrow.

Step 4

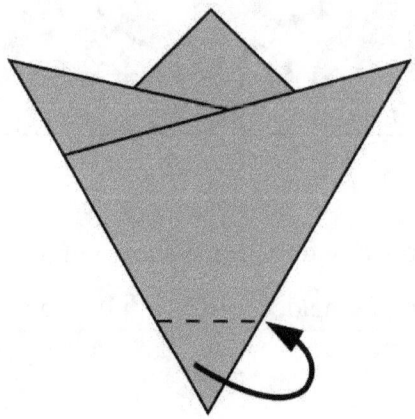

Take the point that's facing you and fold it behind the flower.

Step 5

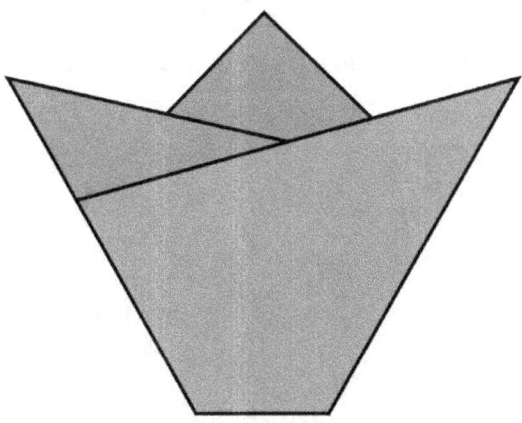

Your flower is finished! Well, not quite. It doesn't have a stem!

Step 6

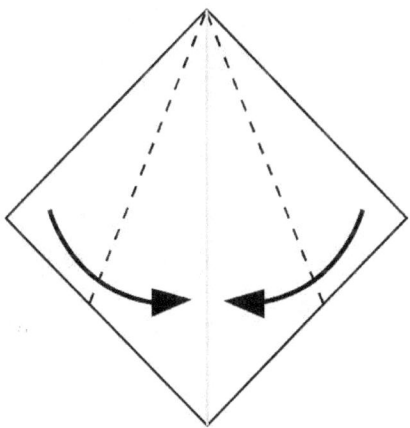

Get a second square of paper and place it on the table with a corner facing away from you. Fold it in half straight down the middle, top to bottom. Unfold it. Then make two more folds along the dotted lines. You made this fold before when learning the peacock.

Step 7

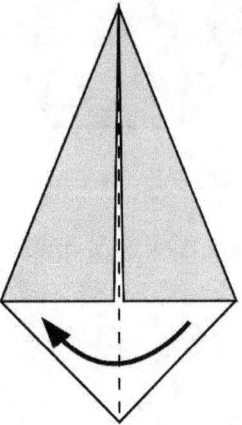

Fold the paper down the middle again, bringing the right corner over to the left corner.

Step 8

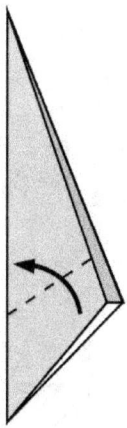

Make a fold along the dotted line shown and bend the paper in the direction of the arrow.

Step 9

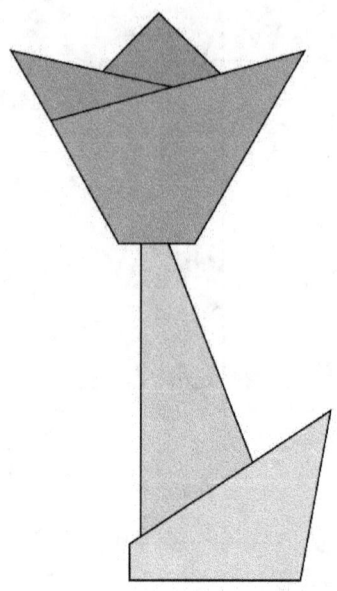

You're almost there.

All you have to do now is insert the top of the stem into the bottom of the tulip flower.

You're done!

Chapter Fifteen: A Whale

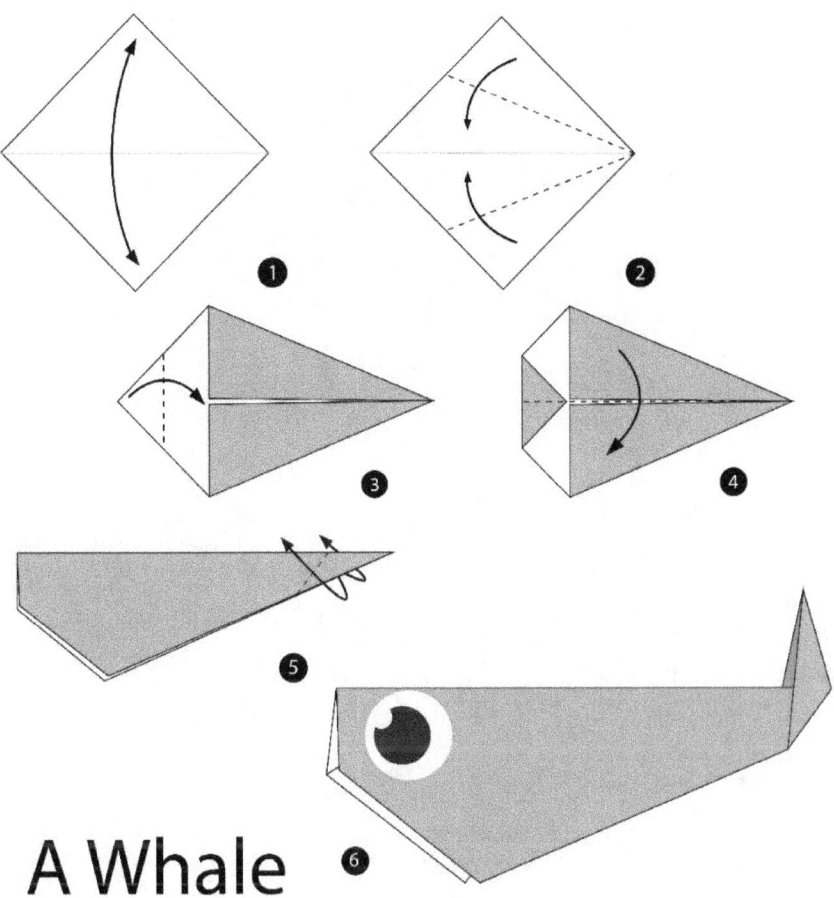

As an island, Japan has a long history of living off the bounty of the sea. There are a lot of whales in the waters around Japan, and the Japanese people have always felt a closeness to them (and often used them for food). Here's a cute and easy design of that giant of the ocean—the whale.

Step 1

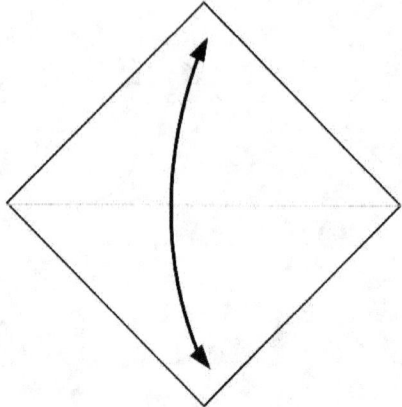

Place the paper flat on the table, and make sure that one of the corners is facing away from you. Fold the paper in half as shown in the picture. Then unfold it.

Step 2

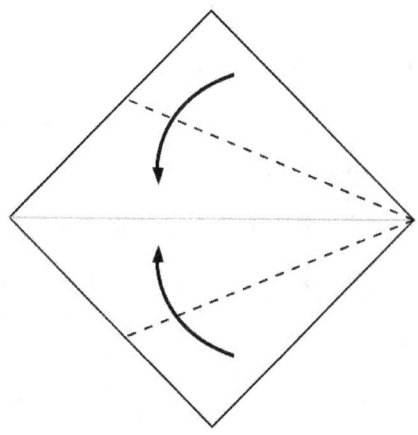

These are folds that you've made before and should be comfortable with by now. Take the top corner (the one facing away from you) and fold it so that its top right side is even with the crease from **Step 1** (that crease is represented by the solid gray line). Now do the same thing from the bottom. Take the bottom corner (the one facing you) and fold it up so that its left side is even with the crease from **Step 1**.

Step 3

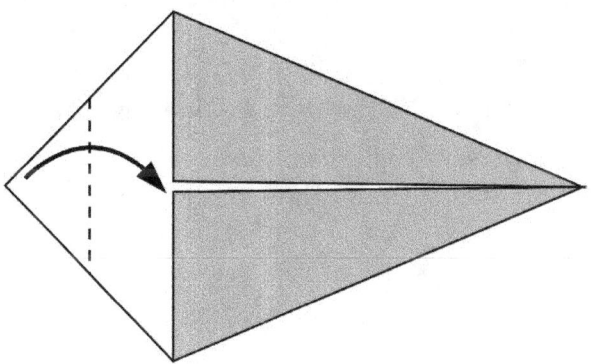

Rotate the paper so that the longest point is facing to the right, as shown in the picture above. At this stage, the shape of your paper somewhat resembles an arrowhead.

Take the point that's facing left and fold it along the dotted line you see in the picture. The point that was facing left should now almost be touching the two flaps.

Step 4

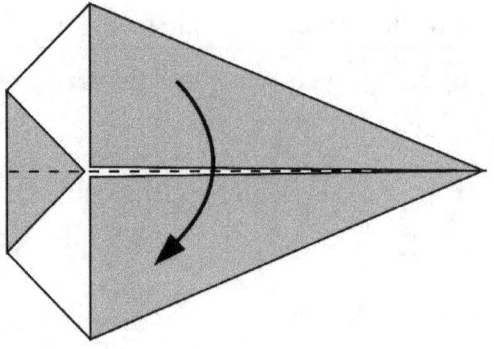

This kind of looks like you're building a paper airplane again, doesn't it?

Fold the paper in half as shown in the drawing. Bring the top half and fold it over the bottom half.

Step 5

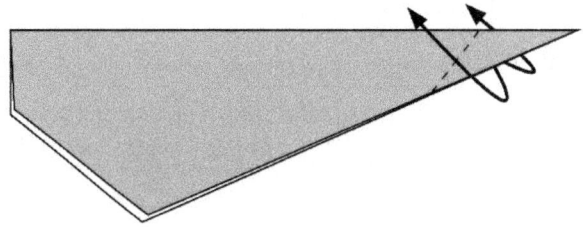

Now you're going to make what's called an outside reverse fold.

Do you see the dotted line in the drawing? Fold the paper along that line. First fold it to the left, then fold it to the right. Make sure you have a good crease.

Now partially unfold the paper and flip the flap over, following the direction of the arrows in the drawing.

Step 6

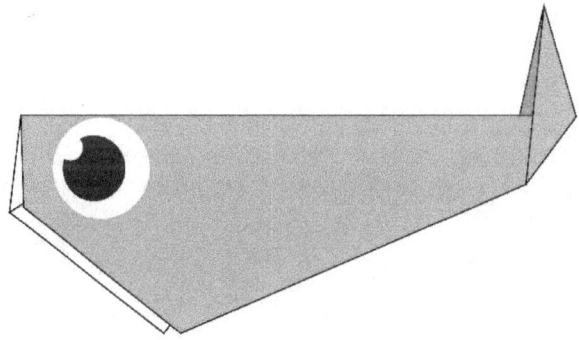

By making an outside reverse fold, you have given your whale a tail! The only thing left to do is give him—or her—an eye. You can draw one with a dark magic marker, or you can glue on a plastic googly eye. And you're done!

Chapter Sixteen: A Brachiosaur

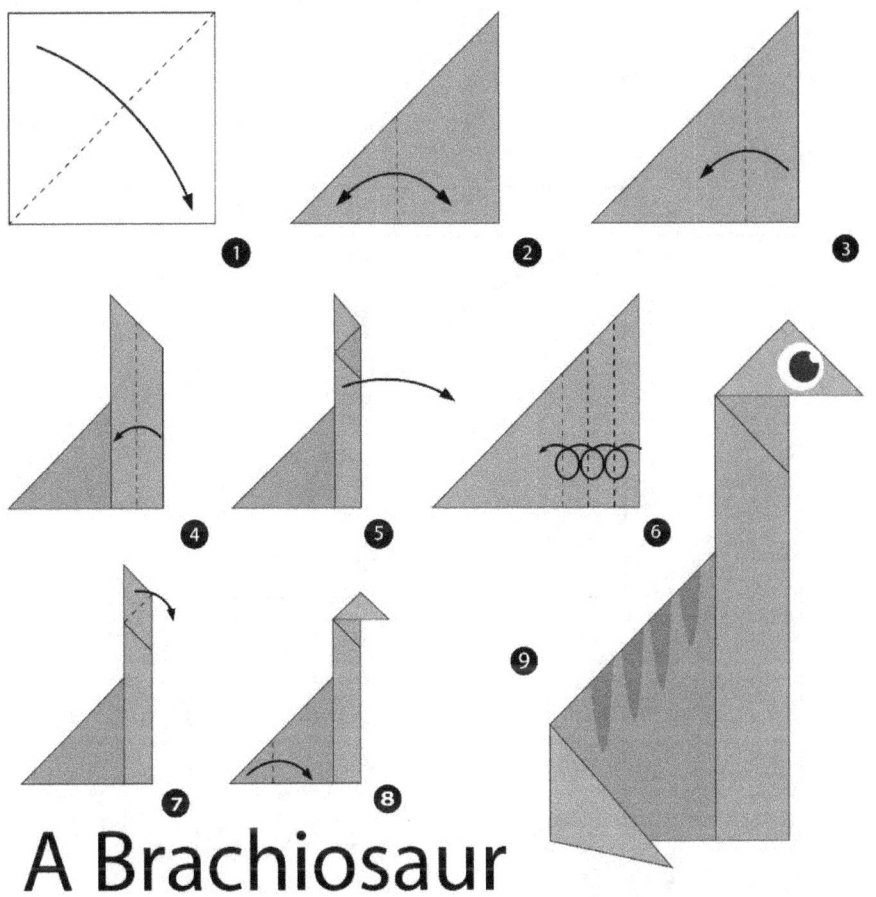

Unlike the other animals you've made so far, the brachiosaur no longer exists. They disappeared from earth millions and millions of years ago, though scientists aren't exactly sure why. Brachiosaurs were *huge*: they were around 80 feet long and weighed more than 60 tons!

But unlike the aggressive tyrannosaurs, the brachiosaurs were very gentle and ate grass and vegetables. They were actually kind of cute for a dinosaur, which is why we're going to make one now.

Step 1

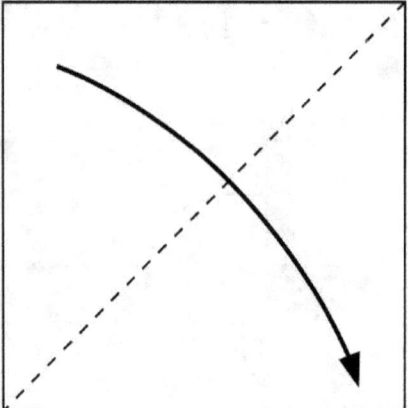

Lay the paper flat on the table. None of the corners should be facing towards you or away from you. Fold the paper in half as shown in the drawing. Take the top left corner and fold it, following the direction of the arrow, till it meets the bottom right corner.

Step 2

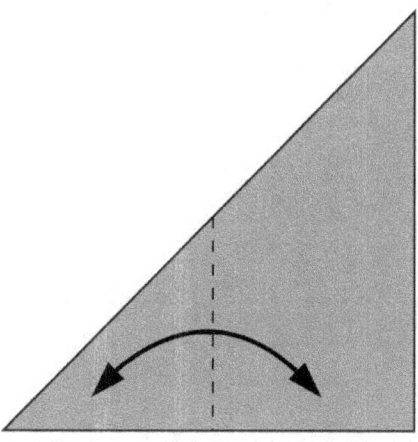

Now you're going to fold the new bottom left corner as shown in the picture. Fold it, then unfold it. Make sure there's a good crease.

Step 3

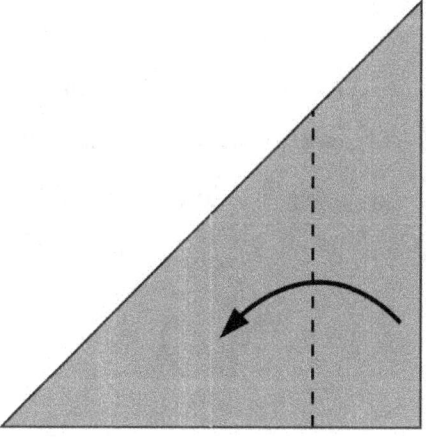

Make another fold, this time from the right. Fold the right side of the triangle so that its edge is even with the crease you made in **Step 2**.

Step 4

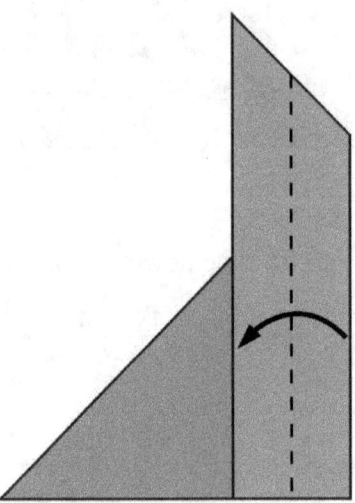

Take a look at the dotted line in the drawing. It sits halfway between the crease you made in **Step 2** and the new right side of your paper. Basically, you're going to fold the right side of your paper till it, too, is even with the crease you made in **Step 2**. You're doubling the fold.

Step 5

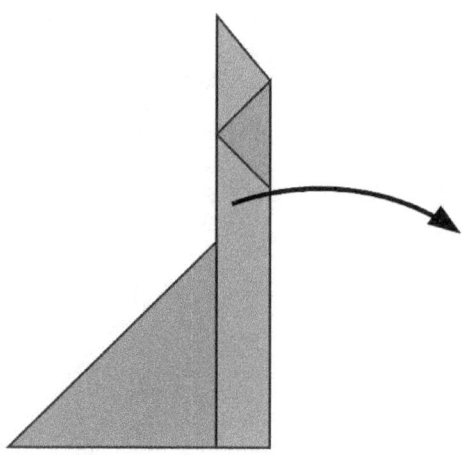

Unfold your paper and lay it out flat so you can see it.

Step 6

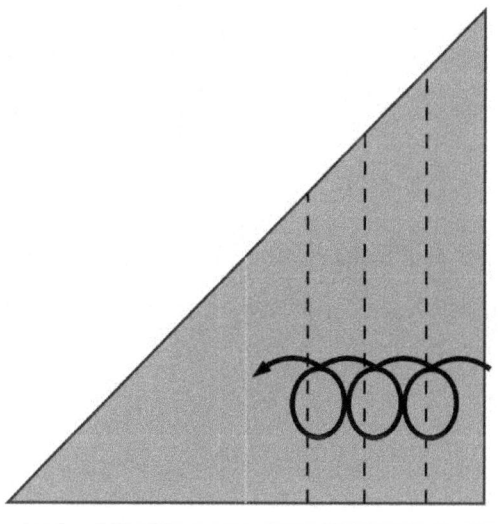

You can now see what you've done: you've made a series of folds across the paper. Make sure the crease of each fold is sharp.

Now refold the paper so that it resembles the figure you had at the beginning of **Step 5**.

Step 7

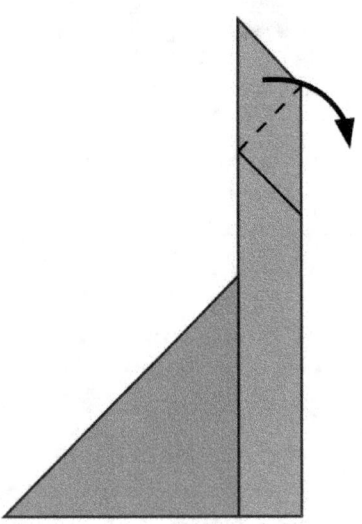

Fold the paper along the dotted line you see in the drawing. This will bring the point of the corner down so that it faces to the right. This will be the face of the brachiosaur.

Step 8

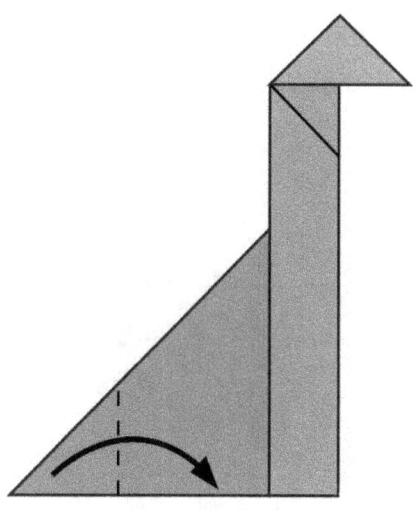

The only fold remaining will create the tail. Take the left corner and fold it to the right. Make sure the crease is good and crisp, because the brachiosaur's tail will need to sit at an angle. The angle will allow the brachiosaur origami to stay upright when you place it down on a table or other flat surface.

Step 9

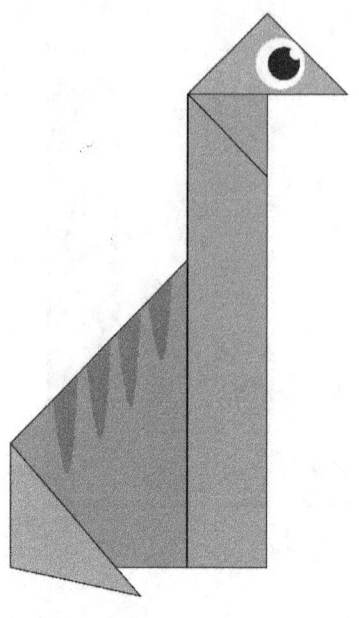

  The only thing left to do is to give your brachiosaur a googly eye and, if you want, some patterns on its back. You can take one of your magic markers and follow the design in the picture, or you can come up with one of your own. It's entirely up to you!

  And you're done! Well, except for naming your new pet…

Chapter Seventeen: A Crane

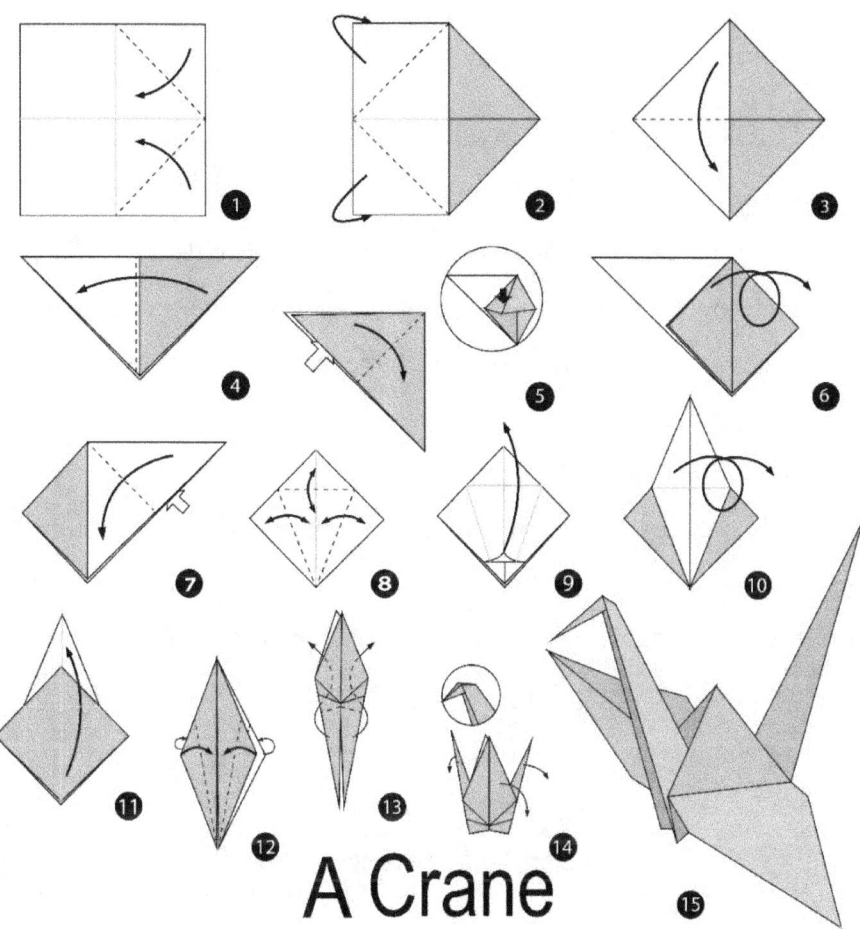

We come, at last, to the crane.

I've saved this origami figure for last because it's so very important in Japanese culture. In fact, it's so important that I want to take a minute and tell you about it before we start making one. This will be one of the most difficult patterns you will ever try. It is very complex…but also very beautiful. You will probably make a lot of mistakes and have to start over a few times. That's okay. Everybody does. Your hard work will be worth it, though.

The Crane in Japanese Culture

For the Japanese, cranes are elegant, mystical birds. For thousands of years, they've treasured the crane as a symbol of honor and loyalty. Hundreds of years ago, the Japanese believed that cranes lived for a thousand years. Because of this belief, the crane came to be seen as a sign of good luck and a long life in Japanese culture.

In Japan, the crane is known as "the bird of happiness." A long time ago, people believed that the wings of the crane carried souls to paradise. Even today, mothers who pray for the protection of their children will offer the following prayer:

O flock of heavenly cranes,
Cover my child with your wings…

Just over 200 years ago, one of the first books about origami was published in Japan. It was called *How to Fold 1,000 Cranes*. You're probably wondering: Why would anyone want to fold 1,000 origami cranes? That's a good question—and it has a surprising answer.

Traditionally, people in Japan believed that if someone folded 1,000 origami cranes, then anything that person wished for would come true. Because of this belief, cranes became not only a symbol of honor and loyalty, but also a symbol of hope and healing during tough times. As a result, a beautiful custom developed and remains to this day: people fold 1,000 paper cranes and string them together—usually there are 25 strings, and each string has 40 cranes. These are then given as gifts. The Japanese love the idea of 1,000 hand-folded cranes so much that they even have a name for it: *senbazuru*.

Cranes as a Symbol of Marriage

In Japan, cranes have become a symbol of marriage. Folding a crane takes time, patience, and understanding, just like marriage. Weddings in Japan are often decorated with 1,000 hand-folded cranes. Even more amazing is that the 1,000 cranes are hand-folded by the people getting married!

Now that you have some idea just how important cranes—and origami cranes, in particular--are, let's make one of our very own!

Step 1

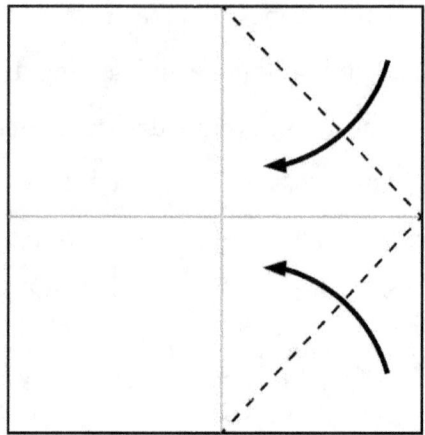

Here we go! Place the square flat on the table. There should be no corners pointing toward you. Fold the paper in half from side to side, then fold it up and down. Unfold your paper and smooth it flat on the table. You should have creases in your paper where the solid gray lines are in the drawing above.

Now take the bottom right corner and fold it toward the center of the paper. The point of the corner should touch the center of the paper. Do the same thing with the upper right corner.

Step 2

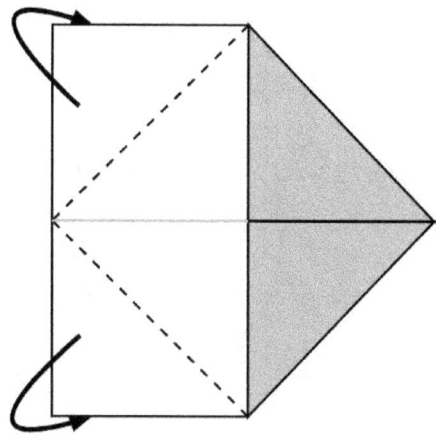

Now for this next move, you're going to do something similar to what you did in in **Step 1**, but you're going to do it in the *opposite* direction.

Take the bottom left corner and fold it toward the center of the square—but fold it *behind* the paper. Now do the same thing with the upper left corner

Step 3

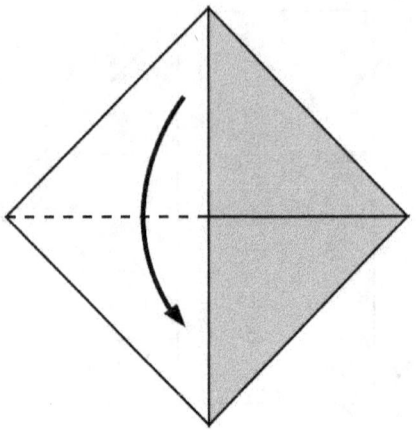

Fold the entire thing in half, bringing the top corner down to meet the bottom corner.

Step 4

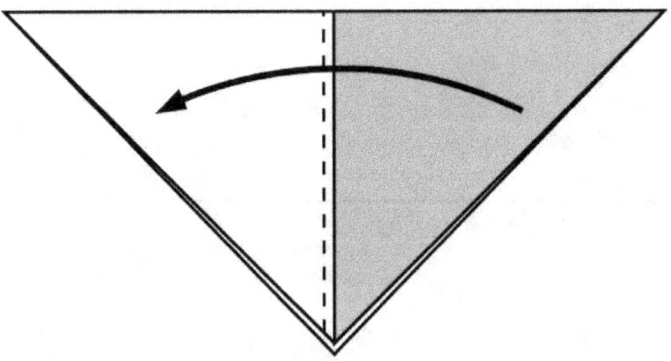

Fold it in half again, but this time fold from right to left.

Step 5

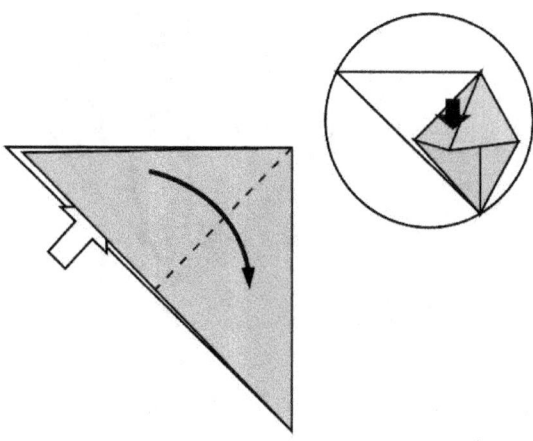

Now, this step here can get tricky. We now have two flaps. A top flap and a bottom flap. Notice the white arrow in the picture? This is where the top flap is. Take the top flap and open it, creasing the left and right sides so you can fold the top left corner to the bottom corner.

If you are still finding it difficult, grab the top part of the flap from where the dotted line starts on the left. You then want to pull it horizontally, across over to the right to get the flap to open up and fold over like the picture below.

Step 6

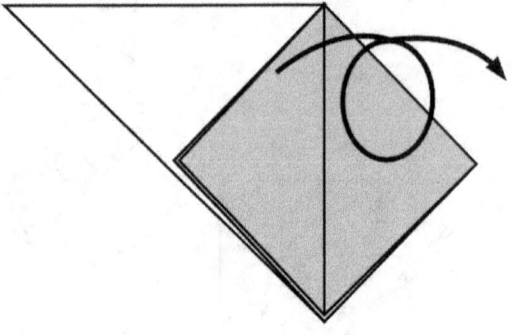

Now turn the paper over.

Step 7

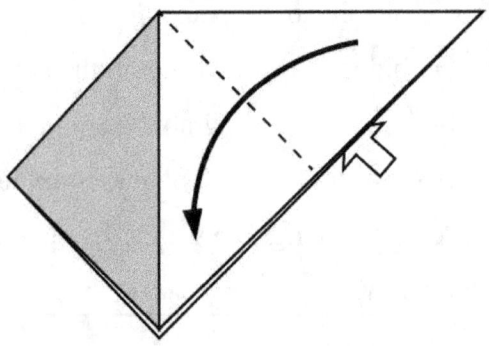

Here, we are going to repeat **Step 5**. Remember, this is the tricky one again. We're not folding the top right corner to the bottom corner. We are opening the flap from the start of the dotted line and pulling it over to the left corner. Read Step 5 again if you are having trouble. You should now have a pretty little square like the picture below.

Step 8

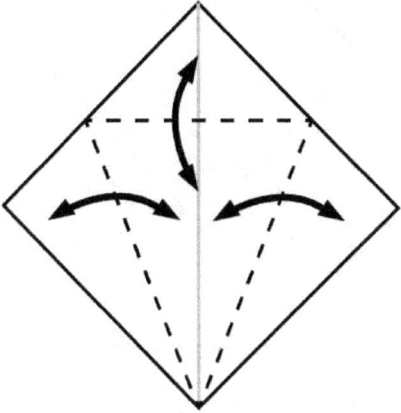

Take both left and right sides of the top layer and fold them in to meet at the middle, then unfold them. We then, want to fold the top corner down like in the picture above and unfold it. This step is preparation for what comes next.

Step 9

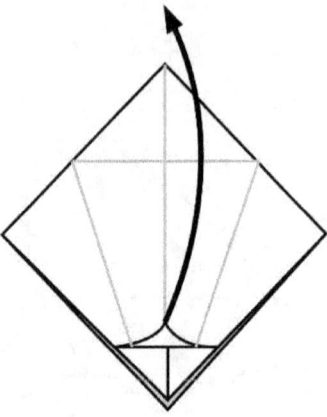

Open the flap upwards. You're going to make what's known as a petal fold. As the flap opens up, you want the bottom corner to meet the top corner and you should notice the flap to open up like a kite shape. You then want to flatten the left and right sides with the top corner so it is now smooth.

Step 10

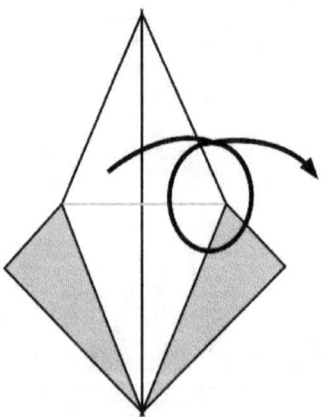

Once you have opened the flap and flattened it into a kite-looking shape, flip the paper over.

Step 11

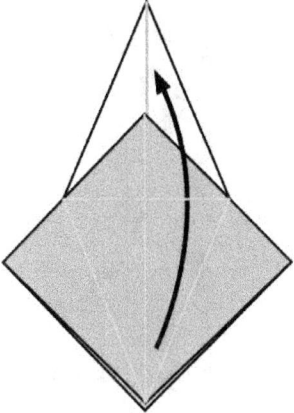

You're going to make the same petal fold on this side, too. So, you will be repeating **Step 9**. Take the top flap and pull it upwards to the top corner as pictured in the drawing above and flatten everything out.

Step 12

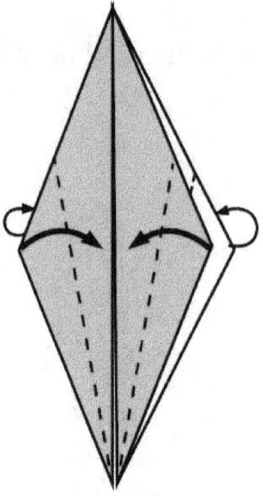

Your paper now looks like this. Congratulations! That part was hard!

Take the left and right corners of the top layer and fold toward the center of the piece. Not all the way to the center, but very close. Do this for the right and left sides.

Flip over and do the exact same thing for the other left and right corners. You should now have an even skinnier kite-looking shape.

Step 13

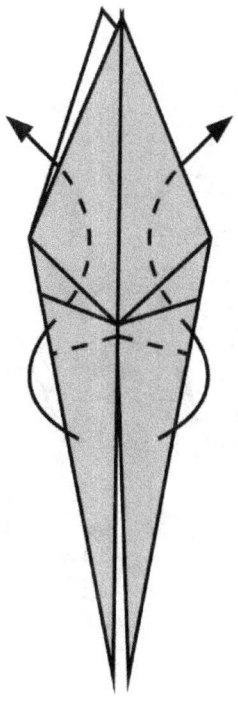

In this step, you're going to make two outside reverse folds with the flaps that are facing you. One will be for the head of the crane and the other will be for the tail of the crane. When you are done, the figure should resemble the drawing in **Step 14**.

Step 14

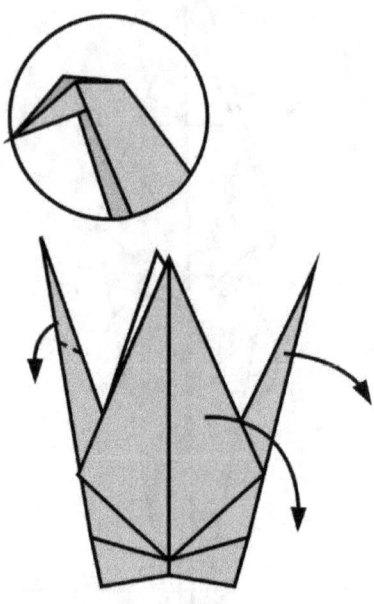

Firstly, flip the paper over. As you can see, everything is pointing up. We need to make our crane look like a crane! The two big flaps opposite each other are the crane's wings. Following the direction of the arrows in the drawing, pull the wings down slightly so that they're even with the floor.

On the right and left side of the drawing, you'll see the tail and head of your crane. Gently pull down the head and tail, but only slightly. You don't want them to be level with the crane's wings. You want the head and tail to stick up a bit.

On the head, you're going to do another outside reverse fold to give the crane a beak.

Step 15

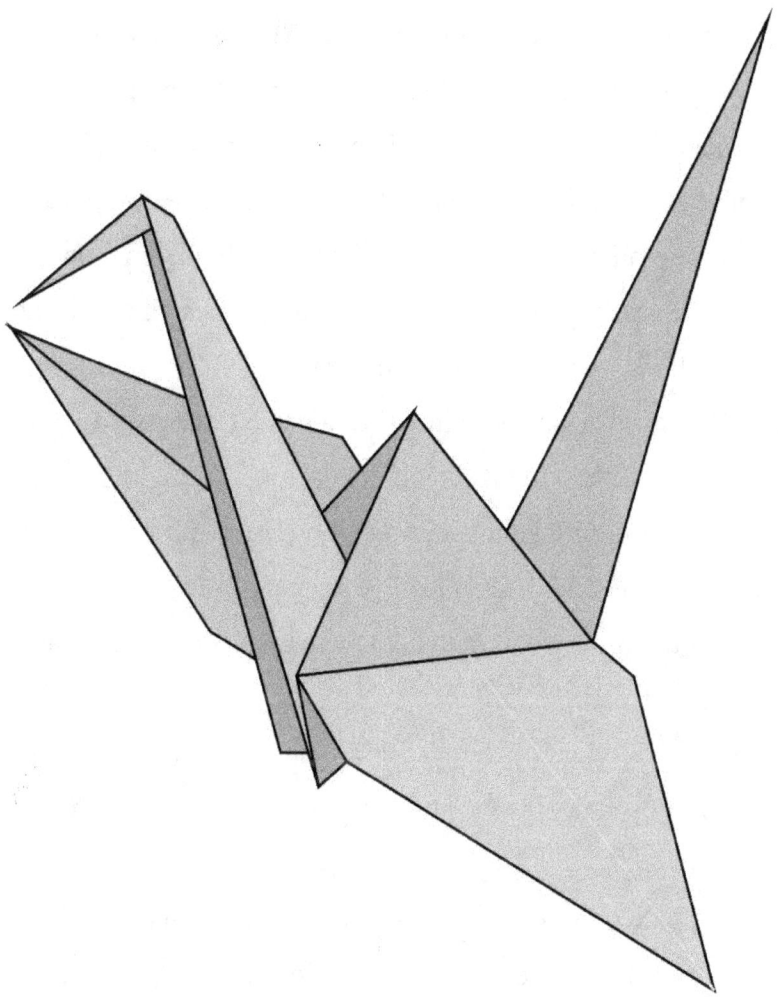

The bird of happiness

Your crane, the bird of happiness, is now complete!

Final Words

I want to thank you for taking the time to make your way through my book. I hope it has given you a good introduction to the ancient art of origami, and that it has made you hungry to seek out more.

Before I go, I thought you might be interested in learning just a little about the man who made origami famous. Although no one persona can be said to have invented origami, one person did make origami popular in our time: Akira Yoshizawa.

Akira Yoshizawa was born in 1911. When he was only 13 years old, he moved to Tokyo to take a job in a factory. When he was in his early 20s, he was promoted to a new position that required him to train new workers. As a child, he had learned origami from his mother. He now taught it to his co-workers to help them understand their machines and how they worked.

During World War II, Akira Yoshizawa got sick and had to spend a long time in a hospital. He made origami models to cheer up the other sick patients.

By now, he was becoming famous for his beautiful origami. In 1951, a Japanese magazine asked him to fold some models for an article about origami. He did, and suddenly he became even more famous. He eventually published 18 books about origami.

Akira Yoshizawa's incredible skill allowed him to travel the world and get people interested in origami. The Japanese government asked him to be a special ambassador, and in 1983 named him to the Order of the Rising Sun, one of the highest honors for a citizen of Japan. He died in 2005, when he was 94.

One of the most amazing things about Akira Yoshizawa is that he was a self-taught origami artist. And by that, I mean that he didn't just follow other people's designs—he made up entirely new designs of his own. His designs were complicated and beautiful and were shown in art galleries around the world. It is said that he created over 50,000 different origami models during his life.

He never used scissors or glue when creating his origami designs. One thing he did do, though, was create a new way of folding. It is called wet-folding, which means that the paper is dampened slightly before making a fold. Wet-folding allows the paper to be folded and bent more easily, and this means that the finished models have a rounder appearance and look more like sculpture. This was something entirely new in origami. No one had ever done it before. By the way, wet-folding requires thicker paper than traditional origami. Regular origami paper is usually very thin and will tear if wet-folding is tried.

I just wanted you to know a little about Akira Yoshizawa. He is the main reason that origami started to become popular in America after World War II. A lot of people never would have heard of origami had it not been for Akira Yoshizawa.

The world is a beautiful place. Sometimes, we get so busy that we miss it. Origami has allowed me to be still and to focus on the beauty of the world and all the things in it. The simplicity of this art is soothing to me, and I hope it has been—and will continue to be—for you, too.

But most of all, I hope you have fun!

Origami Instruction Book for Kids Animals Edition

Fun and Easy Projects for Beginners and Adults Too

Ben Mikaelson

Introduction

Congratulations on downloading *"Origami Instruction Book for Kids Animals Edition: Fun and Easy Projects for Beginners and Adults too."* You are about to embark on an incredible adventure! Perhaps you've already joined me in *"Origami for Kids: Easy Japanese Origami Instruction Book for Kids"* - this was the first book in the series. If not, don't worry! You'll find that this book is just as fun, and just as easy to follow along. The first book covered a variety of projects, while this book covers animals of all kinds. So, if you're a fan of origami and animals, this is certainly the book for you.

There is something very fun and special about taking a simple piece of paper and transforming it into something admirable. In this book, we'll be learning to make colorful, sweet, and even fierce animals (lions, tigers and bears, oh my!). You can make your favorites or make them all and have yourself your very own paper jungle. Whatever you decide, you'll find that each project here is easy to follow, beautiful, and most of all, fun! There are little hidden treasures throughout the book, like fun facts about Japan, and all kinds of cool things about our animal friends. Some of our buddies here are a bit more difficult to make, but if you're not an origami expert, don't worry! Just like in the first book of the series, these projects progress from easiest to the more difficult, so take your time and enjoy the adventure from the start. By the time you get to the end of the book, you'll certainly be an animal origami expert.

Coming up are some instructions (with pictures!) on the different folding symbols, and the different kinds of folds we will be making in our origami projects. You can look back to these sections if you happen to forget, or if you just need some extra help. You'll also be learning how to make a square sheet of paper from a rectangular one, so that you'll be able to use just about any kind of paper you have around the house. That means you'll have a larger variety of colors and patterns to choose from. Your animals are going to be amazing and certainly unique!

There are many books available about origami. I'm greatly appreciative you've chosen to join me for this one, thank you! I sincerely hope you enjoy reading and making each design here. If you find even one moment in which you're smiling, then my job is done. Share some happiness with friends and family by giving these projects as gifts, teaching someone else how to do origami, or even reading this book with others and learning to do origami together. It's a lot of fun to do with others! Are you ready to get started? I hope so! Here we go…

Chapter 1: All About Origami

Before we get to folding and creating our animal works-of-art, let's talk a bit about what origami is, and where it came from. Maybe this is your first time reading about origami. Maybe you've read about it before, like in the first book in this series: *Origami for Kids: Easy Japanese Origami Instruction Book for Kids*. Either way, it's good to brush up your knowledge and maybe even learn something new.

Origami (said like or-i-gah-me) is the Japanese work for paper folding. "Ori" means "to fold" and "gami" (kami in Japanese) means "paper". Put them together, and you have "origami" which is "to fold paper", of course. I know you already figured that out. Origami is an art form that has evolved and travelled through generations (from adults passed on to kids like you, and when those kids are all grown up, they pass it on to kids, and it just keeps going) throughout Japan. I know, you probably already knew that too. But what you may not know is that origami actually *started* in China, not Japan. Paper was *very* expensive back then, so only people with a lot of money used it, and some very wealthy emperors would practice origami as an art, and be given paper and origami as gifts.

After a while, paper became more affordable, and then everyone was using it for all kinds of things. Origami became more and more popular, mostly in Japan, and they really began to make some amazing things. Japan really made origami what it is today. Since that is where it evolved and gained popularity, even though it may have started in China, it's an important part of Japanese culture. Origami is usually taught at home as part of Japanese tradition.

Origami is more than just art...

So now you know where origami started and how it gained its popularity and spread to Japan. While there are beautiful, elaborate works of origami that are most certainly works of art, the benefits of origami don't stop there. It is actually very good for our mental and physical health.

Scientists have discovered that doing activities that challenge our mind and build on our existing abilities and talents through a variety of tasks, like puzzles and- you guessed it- origami, can strengthen the brain. Origami is an activity that can provide both mental and physical stimulus with a bit of exercise. Using the hands for direct contact activity helps stimulate certain areas of the brain. Origami helps build and strengthen hand-eye coordination, mental concentration, and fine motor skills. Paper folding is even used in therapeutic causes, like art therapy and stroke and injury rehabilitation.

Since origami has detailed instructions, it challenges us at a cognitive level as we learn to follow these instructions, obtain new skills, and complete new activities. When you engage in origami, impulses are sent to the brain that then begin activating both the left and right hemispheres. The tactile, motor and visual areas of the brain are activated and brought into use. This also stimulates the memory, non-verbal thinking, attention, 3D comprehension and imagination.

Origami also creates added emotional health. When we learn something new and create something (like any of these cool paper animals), we get a sense of satisfaction, pride, and other feel-good emotions. This helps boost creativity, self-esteem, and confidence. All these great things just from simple paper folding.

Chapter 2: What You'll Need

One of the things that makes Origami so special is that you don't need much at all. A simple piece of paper can be transformed, almost like magic, into something entirely new. Who knew that a piece of paper could become a giraffe, a squirrel, a fish, and so much more? I certainly didn't, until I learned all about this amazing art.

The first thing you'll need to get started is some square sheets of paper. Squares and rectangles look kind of alike, so how do you know which one is a square? That's a good question. When the paper is a square, all of the four sides will be the same length. A rectangle has four sides too, but two sides are longer than the other two. Take a look at the picture below, and you'll see what I mean. Just because a sheet of paper is a rectangle, though, doesn't mean you can't use it- you just have to make it into a square first. In just a minute, you'll learn how to do just that.

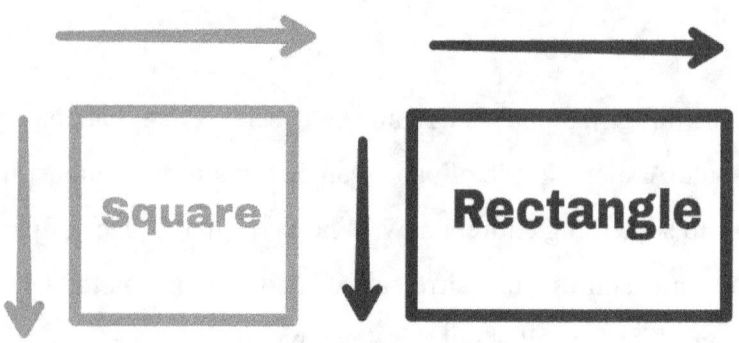

There are specially made papers for origami in all kinds of textures, colors, and patterns, but you really don't need anything fancy, especially to get started and practice. You probably have some paper around the house that is just perfect. Ask an adult to help you track some down if you need to. You can use whatever color or pattern you like. You can even use some plain white paper. Or take some white paper and color it yourself. This is especially nice to use for a gift, plus it adds some extra fun. You can use colorful pages from an old book (with permission, of course!), notebook paper, and lots of other things. Get creative! When you choose your paper, you don't want to use something too thick (like card stock or thick construction paper), because it is pretty hard to fold. You also don't want something too thin (like tissue or wrapping paper) because it tears very easily. Other than that, the sky is the limit, so get creative and go wild!

Once you have some paper, find a flat surface to work on. It doesn't have to be a desk; you can do origami just about anywhere. A coffee table or kitchen table are both great places, and of course a desk is also perfect. You just need a small area of a flat surface to fold on. Even a lap desk will work.

So, do you have your paper, and a place to fold it? Great! Now, some people like to use special tools to help make the folds *very* tight by pressing them down harder, but you don't need to worry about that. Just be sure to press down firmly when you make your folds.

The very last thing you need is maybe some patience. When you learn something new, you might make mistakes, or not understand right away. That's ok! I certainly didn't know these things when I was young, and now here I am making a book to teach you. Maybe you'll make your own book one day! Keep trying and practicing, and soon you'll find that you've got the hang of it. Remember to have patience for others that might be trying to learn with you as well.

Fun Fact: One pine tree can be made into about 80,500 sheets of paper. That's a whole lot of origami!

Chapter 3: How to Make a Square from a Rectangle

Remember when I said you could make a square from a rectangle? Now I'm going to show you how. For this, you *will* need a pair of scissors. If you need some help, ask an adult.

Take a look at the pictures below for each step to making a square. There are just 3 easy steps. First, lay your paper flat.

Step 1

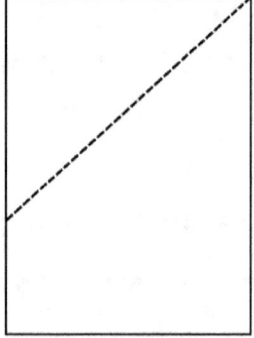

Fold #1: Fold along the dotted line, matching edge to edge.

Step 2

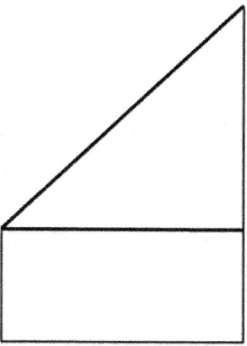

See the bottom section, away from the edge you folded down? Trim that off with your scissors.

Step 3

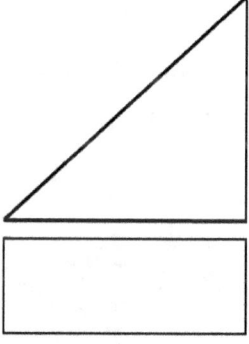

Unfold your paper, and you're done! Now you have a square to work with.

Chapter 4: A Few Folds

There are a few folds in some of these projects that are a little trickier than the basics. Now, you many already know these folds, but just in case, here's some extra help in case you need it. Let's start with the very basics, and work our way up.

Every piece of origami uses what we call a mountain fold, and/or a valley fold. You've made these many, many times with other projects that had nothing to do with origami- that's how common and easy they are.

The Valley Fold: Do you know what a valley is? It's a lower "dip" in the land, which is why this fold is called a valley. For a valley fold, the crease is made by folding the paper upward into itself, creating a "v" shape, or what looks like a "dip" in the paper. Take a look.

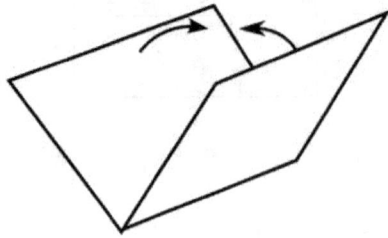

The Mountain Fold: Like a valley is low, a mountain is a high point or peak. The mountain fold is basically the opposite of the valley fold. For a mountain fold, the crease is made at the top, and the paper folded down on to itself, rather that up onto itself, formed and upside down "v". Here's how it looks:

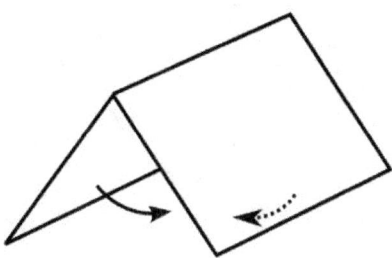

The Squash Fold: The squash fold is a rare one in this book. Only the two projects in this book involves the squash fold. At first it might look kind of hard, but once you understand, it's really not! You may have already done a squash fold before and just not realized what it was called. To make a squash fold, pry open the paper, and then flatten (or squash) it down. Take a look at the set of images below. These pictures show one example of a piece using a squash fold. Your first squash fold will be with the Bear Cub project, so when you get to it, refer back to this section if you need to.

Step 1

Lift the flap that is to be squashed up towards you.

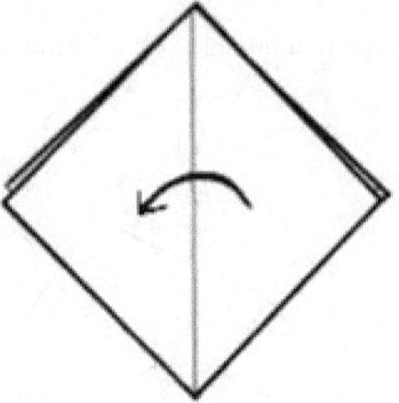

Step 2 and 3

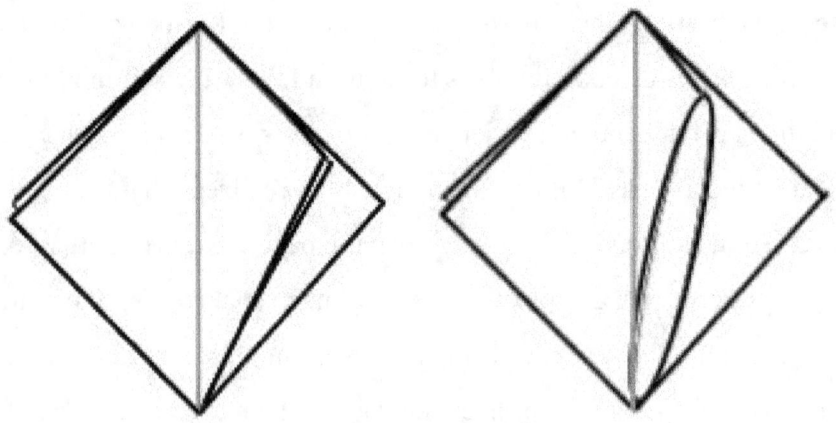

Separate apart the layers of paper.

Step 4 and 5

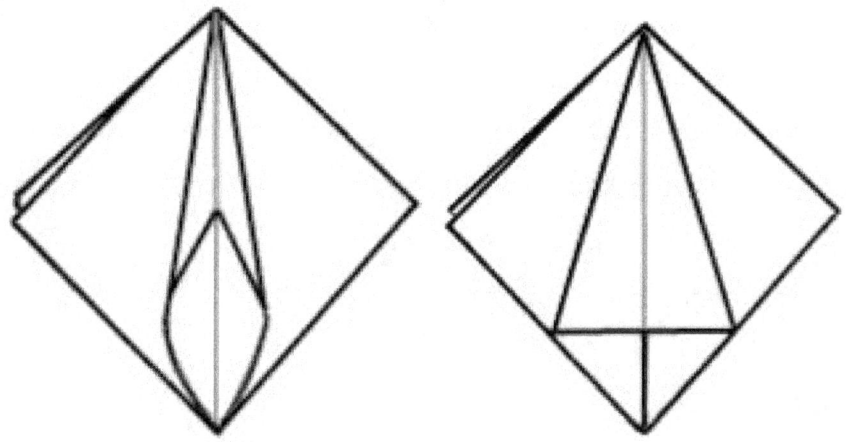

Carefully press down to squash the paper creating two new folds. Align the crease on the top layer of paper with the layers of paper beneath.

The pocket fold: The inside reverse fold, also called the pocket fold, is another common fold made in origami. To make this fold, follow the steps below. The pictures here are to help you understand how the fold works; we're not making anything here, really. We're just learning the different folds and practicing. You can come back to this section whenever you need to.

Step 1

Take a square piece of paper, and fold it in half, so that it looks like the picture below. Then fold along the dotted line, is indicated in the picture as well.

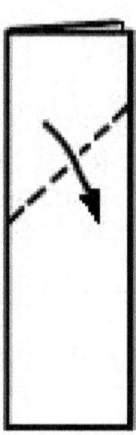

Step 2

The image below is what your paper should look like after step one. Now unfold, shown by the arrow.

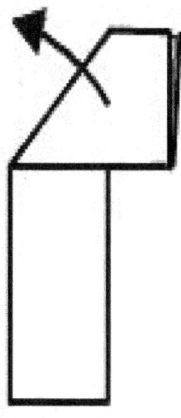

Step 3

See the large black arrow? Fold that corner inward and down along the dotted line, so that it is sandwiched on the inside, like a pocket.

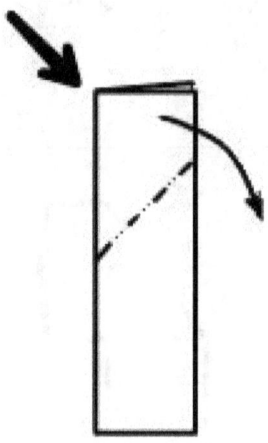

Step 4

The image below is what the final result should look like! Making a crease and then folding the paper to the inside is always the point of a pocket fold, which is what you just did.

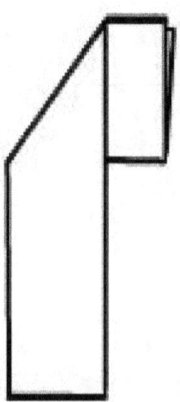

The hood fold: The outside reverse fold, also called the hood fold, is very similar to the pocket fold. Look at the images below to see the differences and similarities.

Step 1

This time, fold your paper in half from right to left. Then fold along the dotted line, as shown by the arrow in the picture below.

Step 2

Now unfold the previous step, as shown below again by the arrow.

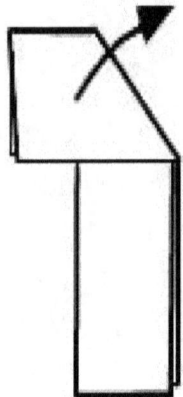

Step 3

Fold again along the dotted line shown below, but this time while opening the paper and pushing the lower half (the section below the dotted line) up and to the inside. Take a look at step 4 to see what I mean, and what it should look like.

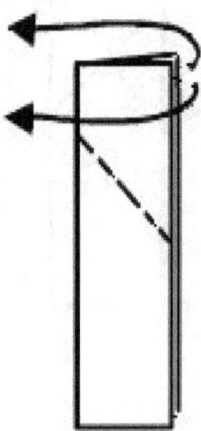

Step 4

This is what your paper should look like when you've completed step 3. Don't forget, you can always ask for help if you're having some trouble. You'll get it in no time!

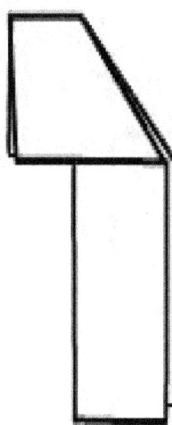

The Stair Fold: just like the other folds here, the stair fold is called that because it resembles the step of a stair. For this, we'll practice on a square piece of paper, just like what we use with all origami.

Step 1

Start with a mountain fold, folding a segment of the paper backwards, where the small dotted line is in the picture below. Turn the paper over (this isn't always required or possible with every origami project, but for learning the fold, it helps!).

Step 2

Using the same segment that you folded backward, make a fold where the thicker dotted line is in the picture below, and return the paper to its original position by turning it over.

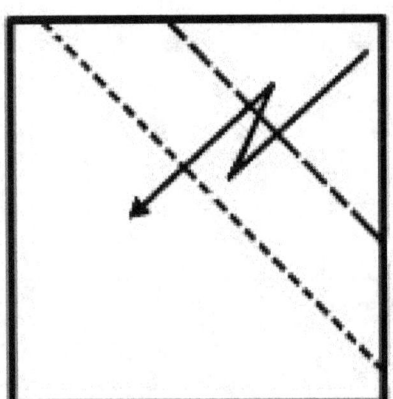 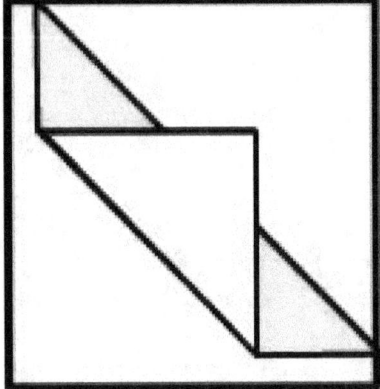

Chapter 5: Symbols for Getting Started

Each project in this book has written instructions as well as pictures to help you fold the very best you can. The pictures also have some special symbols to help you understand what's going on in the pictures. Before we get started on our very first animal friend, I'm going to show you each symbol you might see, and explain what they all mean. Don't worry, it's easier than it sounds!

Here's our first set of symbols:

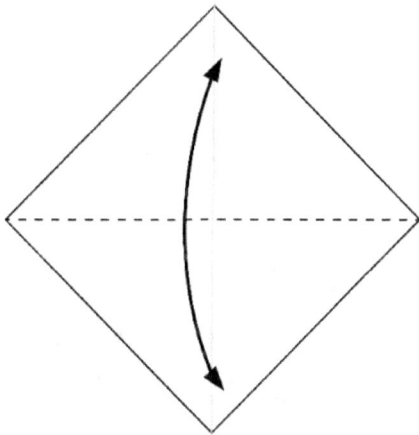

How many symbols do you think you see? There are three here. First, the dotted line in the middle from left to right. See it? A dotted line means this is where you **fold and unfold**. Now, see the solid gray line going from the top to the bottom? You have a good eye! This solid line

153

shows you where the crease of your folds should be. Lastly in this picture, you see an arrow. The arrow shows you in which direction you need to fold.

Now let's look at the next symbol:

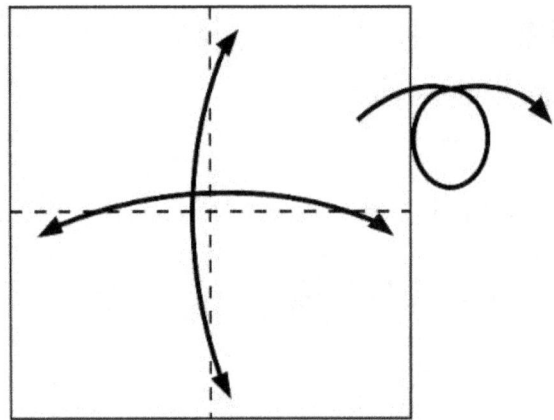

Here, you can see two sets of arrows. Do you remember what those mean? If you think it shows which direction to fold, you're right! Now, see the arrow with a loop? When you see this funny loopy arrow, it means you need to turn the paper to the other side.

There are more symbols to learn as you get better and better, but for now, this is all we need to know to start making adorable and ferocious animals. I hope you are as excited to learn as I am to teach you! Are you ready? Here we go!

Chapter 6: Tiger (Face)

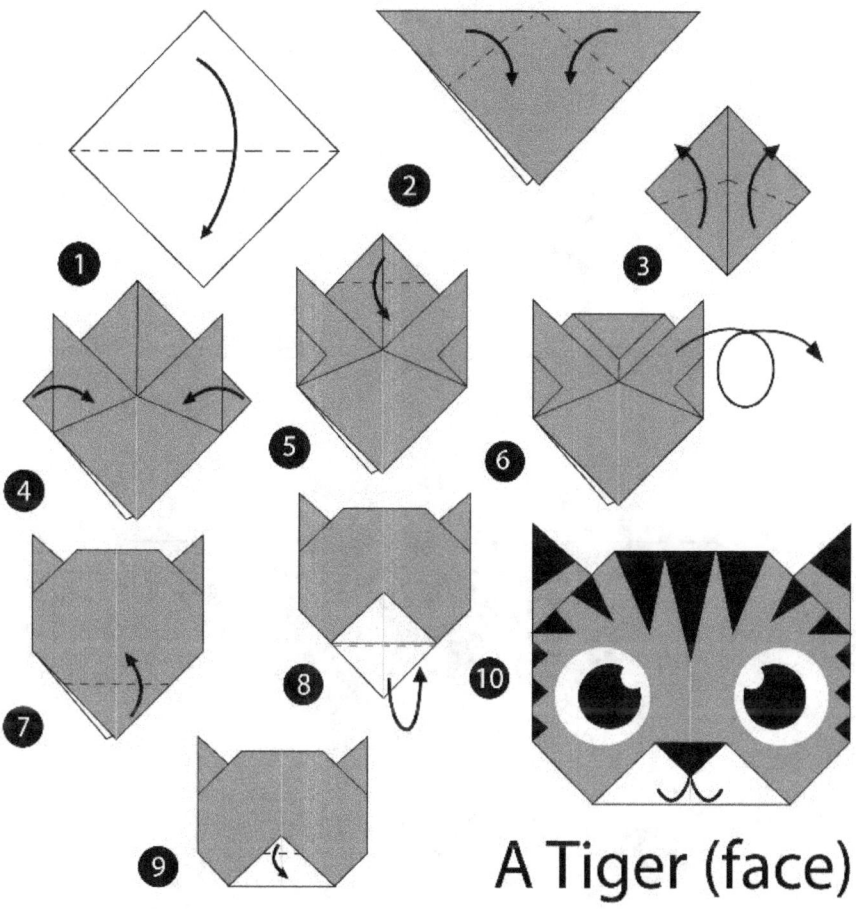

A Tiger (face)

This adorable tiger face is the very first origami project I remember doing! Start off with your paper flat on your work surface with the color or pattern side facing down. If you just have white paper that is fine too.

Step 1

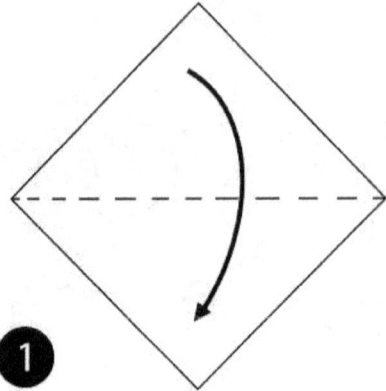

Fold in half from top to bottom, across the dotted lines.

Step 2

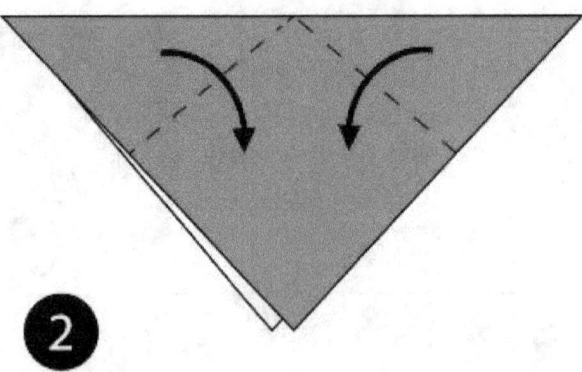

Fold the left point down to the center. Repeat this with the right point, so that they meet in the center. The folds will be where you see the dotted lines.

Step 3

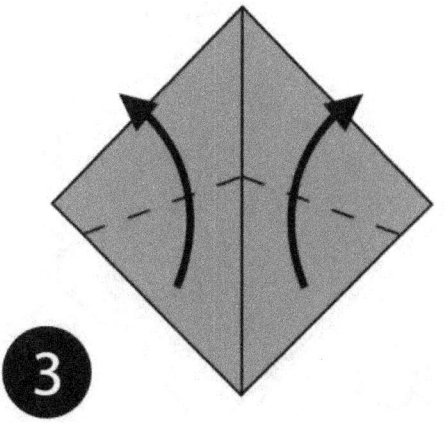

Fold the left point upwards and out a bit towards the left. Repeat this with the right point. You can see what it looks like by looking at the next picture.

Step 4

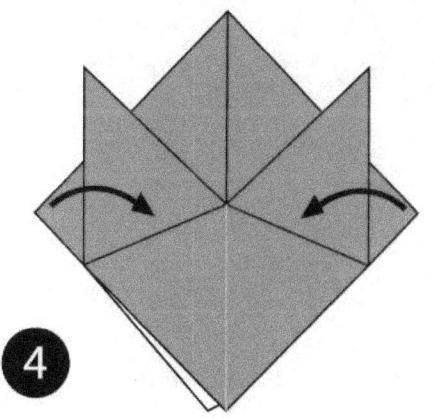

Fold the left point over as shown in the picture. Repeat with the right point. Be sure to crease well.

Step 5

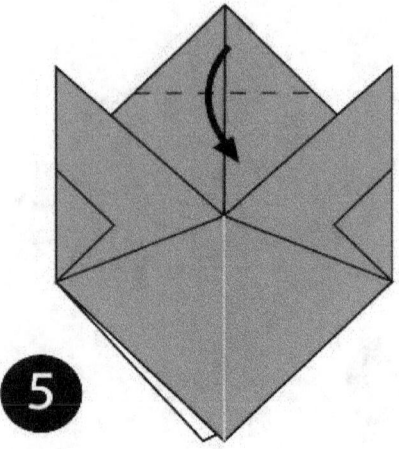

Fold the top point down, following along the dotted line. Crease well.

Step 6

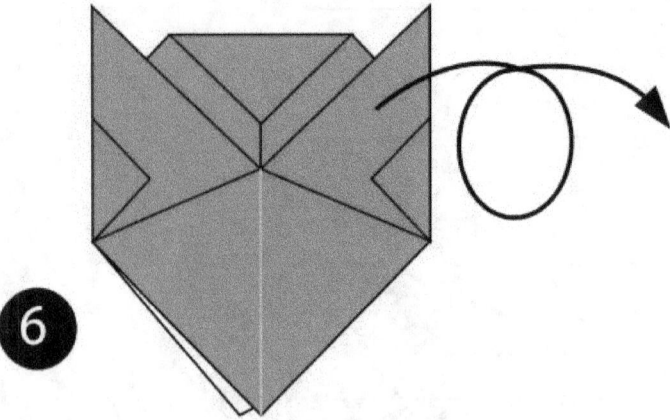

Turn the whole project over, like shown in the picture.

Step 7

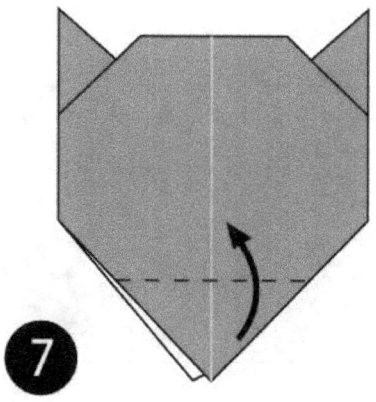

Fold just the top layer of paper (not both layers of paper) upward.

Step 8

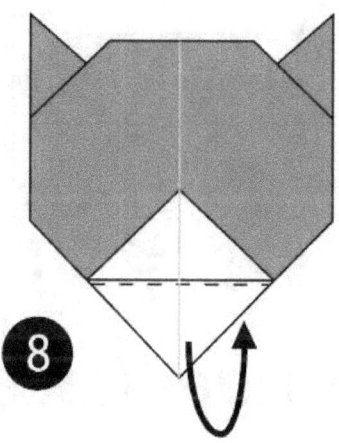

Now you have a point folded up with one layer, and one layer pointing down. Fold the point on the bottom backwards, behind everything. Crease well.

Step 9

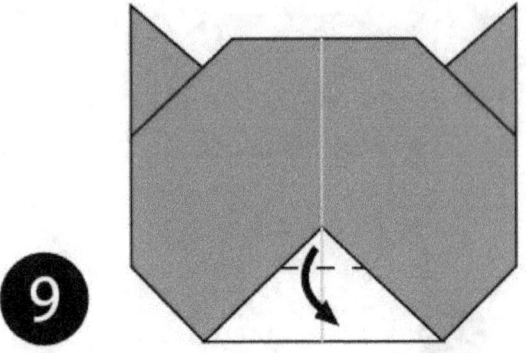

Now fold the tip of the point on top down as shown to make the tiger's nose.

Step 10

A Tiger (face)

You're done folding your tiger face! Now you can add your tiger's stripes, nose, and eyes. You can also decide that maybe this isn't a tiger after all, and color it as a jaguar, black panther, or a house cat.

Fun fact: The tiger is the biggest species of the cat family They can reach a length of up to 11 feet and weigh as much as 660 pounds. That's a big cat!

Did you know… the Japanese word "kami" for paper can also mean "spirit" or "god". This is because origami was originally used in spiritual or religious ceremonies. Nowadays, it's used for all kinds of things.

Chapter 7: Pig (Face)

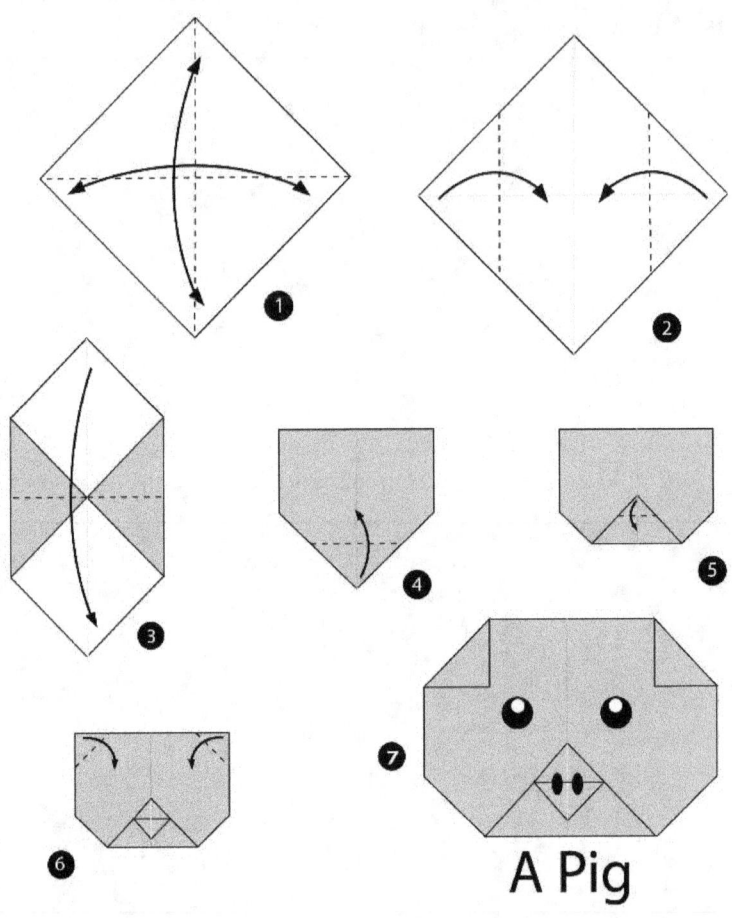

Oink! Oink! Here's another adorable animal face to add to your collection. Just like the tiger, this little piggy is super easy to make. Start with your paper flat on your work surface with the color or pattern side facing down, in the shape of a diamond.

Step 1

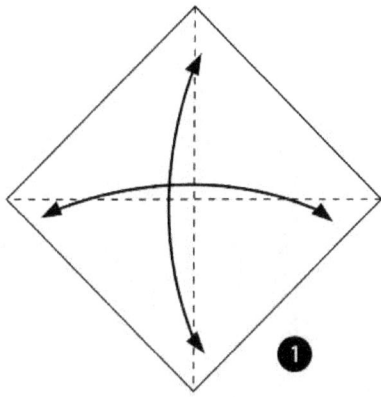

Fold the left corner straight across to the right one, as shown by the dotted line. Crease well, then unfold. *Fold #2:* Fold the bottom corner to the top, where the dotted lines are shown. Crease well and unfold again.

Step 2

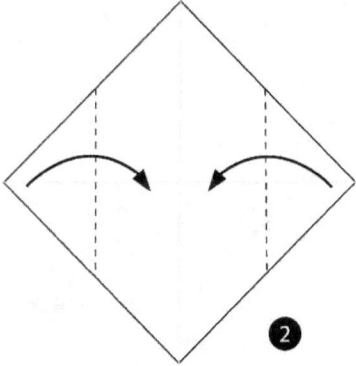

You should now have creases where the solid grey lines are shown in the picture. Fold the left corner over to the center, and crease well. Now fold the right corner the same way, so that they meet in the center.

Step 3

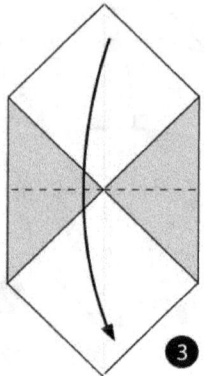

See the arrow in the picture? Fold the top point all the way down to the bottom point, as shown by the arrow. You're folding the project in half.

Step 4

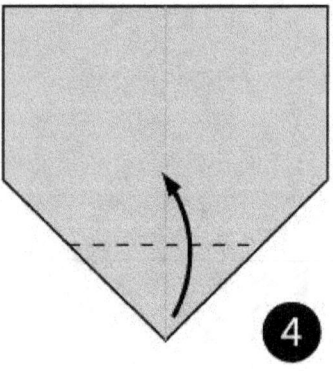

Fold the bottom point up as shown in the picture. Crease well.

Step 5

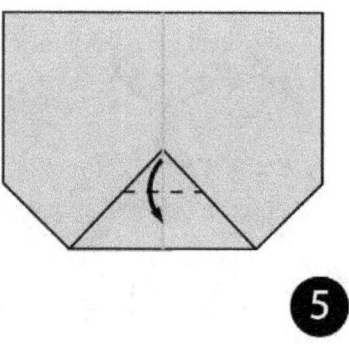

Fold the top point down, as shown in the picture. This is going to be your pig's snout.

Step 6

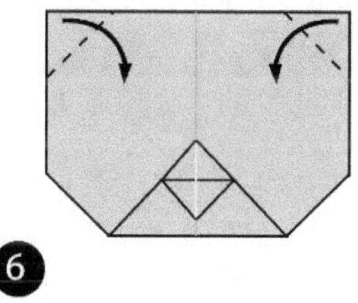

Fold along the dotted line on the left side as shown, and repeat the same thing on the right side. These are the ears.

Step 7

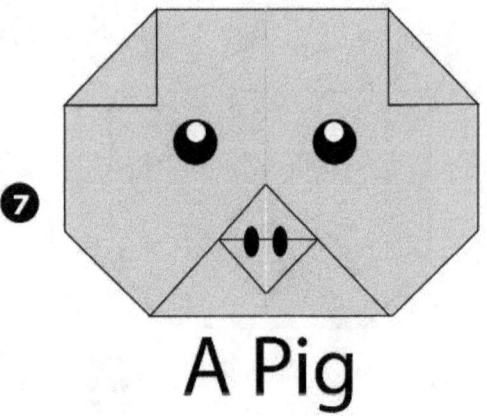

A Pig

And you're done! Now you can give your pig's face some detail by drawing on its eyes and holes on its snout.

Fun Fact: Pigs are one of the most intelligent domesticated animals, even smarter than dogs!

Did you know… paper was first invented in China in 105 CE. It was first made from the hemp plant.

Chapter 8: Bulldog (Face)

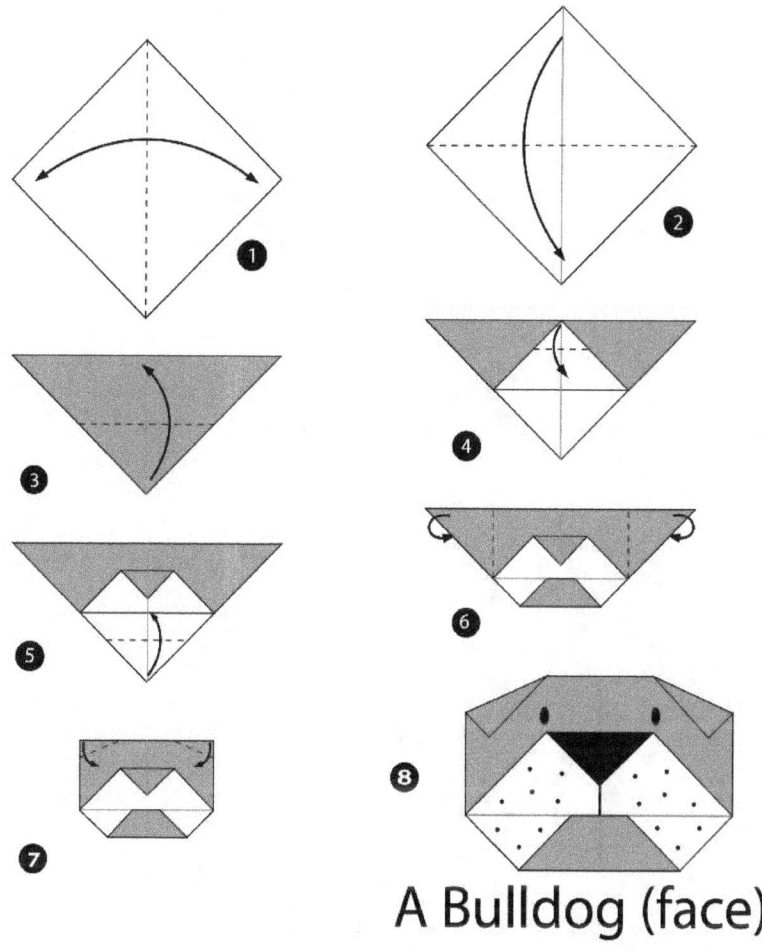

A Bulldog (face)

So far, we have a tiger, a pig and now it's time to add a dog into the mix! And what better dog to add than a bulldog? To make this cutie, start with your paper flat on your work surface with the color or pattern side facing down, and with the paper in the shape of a diamond.

Step 1

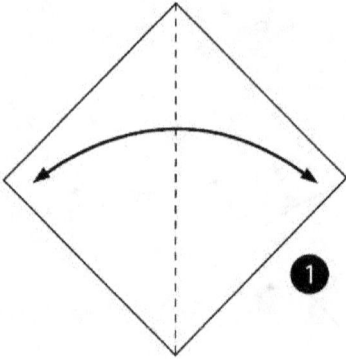

Fold your paper in half along the dotted line as shown, folding it in half from left to right. Crease well, then unfold.

Step 2

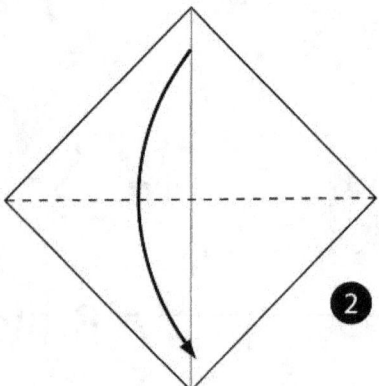

Just as you did in step one, you'll be folding the paper in half here again, but this time folding from top to bottom, as shown. Crease well, and this time leave it folded.

Step 3

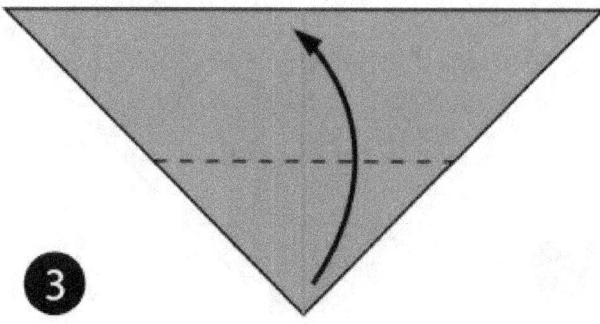

Fold the top layer of the bottom point up so that it touches the top edge. You can see what I mean by looking at the picture in step 4.

Step 4

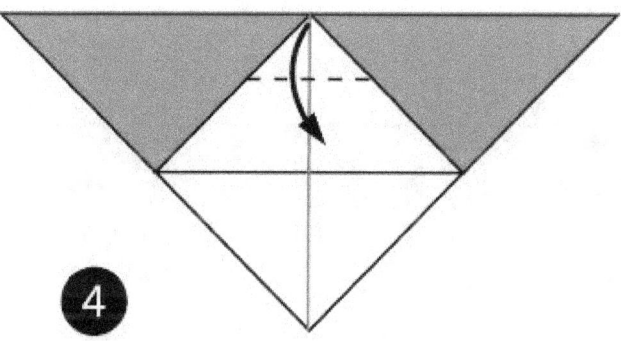

Now fold the top point to the center, as shown by the dotted line.

Step 5

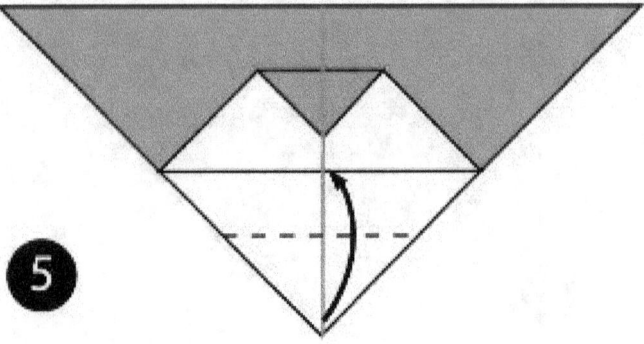

See the dotted line in this step? Fold the bottom point upward along the dotted line as shown, and crease well. And then tuck in a tiny portion of the paper like in the picture below.

Step 6

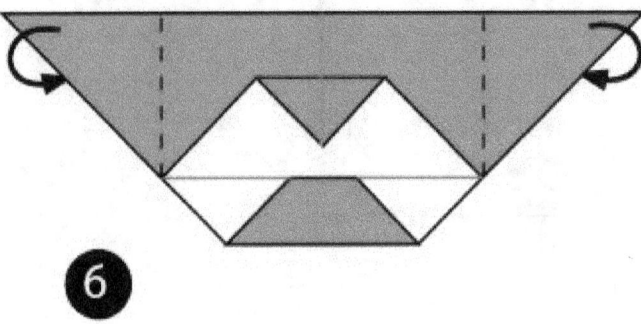

Fold backwards along the dotted line on the left side as shown. Then repeat this same fold on the right side, so that they match.

Step 7

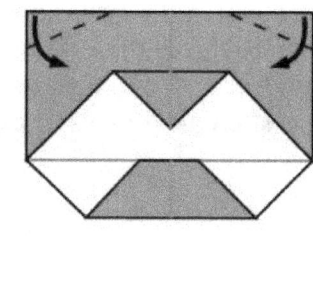

See the dotted lines on both sides? Fold down along them as shown in the picture.

Step 8

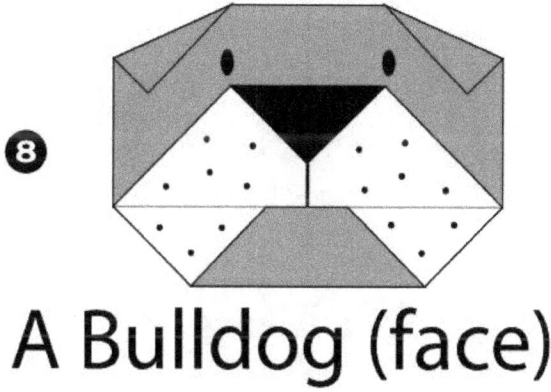

A Bulldog (face)

Your bulldog face is ready to have its features and details drawn on. How will your dog look? Maybe it has sleepy eyes, or ones that are wide awake. Does your dog have a black nose, or a pink one? Maybe it has spots!

Fun Fact: Bulldogs are courageous, loyal, and laid-back, which makes them great furry family members. They are good watch dogs, but also love being close to their family and cuddling.

Did you know... Origami has a strong link to math, and has been used in developing things such as airbags in cars.

Chapter 9: Fish

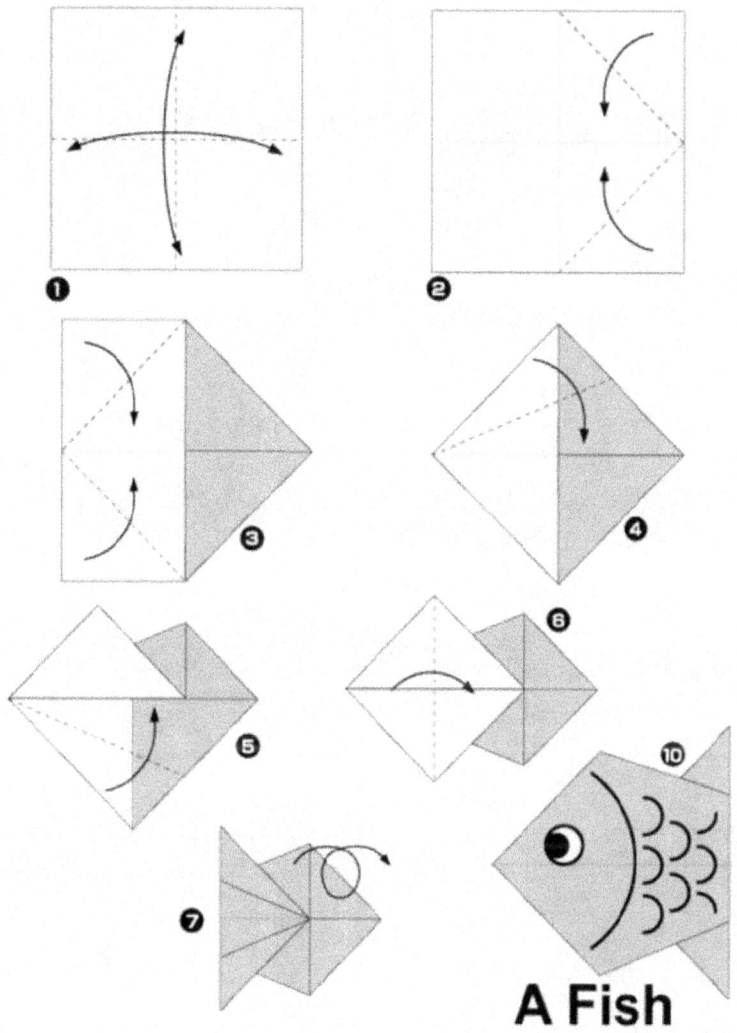

A Fish

Like most projects, start with your paper flat on your work surface, with the color (or pattern) side face down. The color or pattern will be the color of your fish. Position your paper so it is a square.

Step 1

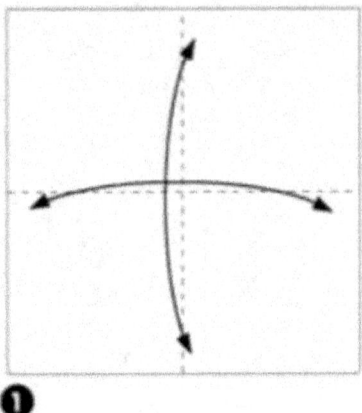

Fold in half from top to bottom, across the dotted lines. Crease well, and unfold. Now fold in half from left to right, crease well, and unfold again. This step is very easy, you're simply making two folds and then unfolding. This is your first step to creating your fish!

Step 2

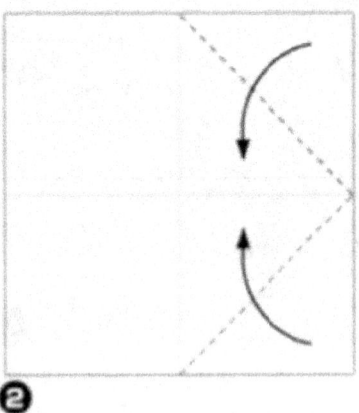

See the solid lines in the picture? You should now have a cross shape in the center of the paper where the creases were formed; these are shown with the grey lines. Fold the lower right corner up to the very center of the cross. Do the same with the upper right corner, by folding the upper right corner to the center as well.

Step 3

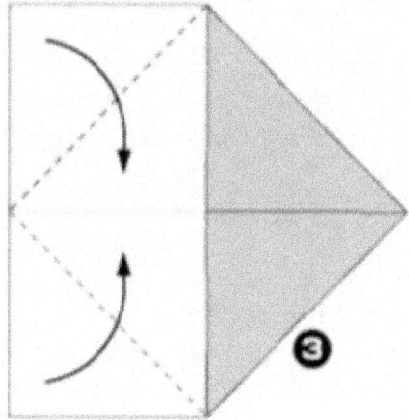

Repeat the third and fourth folds on the left side of the paper, as shown in the picture, but instead of folding them to meet in the front, fold them behind to the center of the cross on the back. Now you should have a folded square that is half one color, half another (if the front and back of your paper is different in color, of course).

Step 4

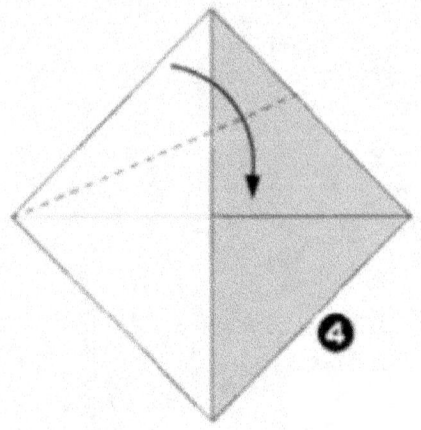

Following the arrow, fold across the dotted line making the edge meet in the middle. This will cause the portion you folded backwards to form a "flap" on the front.

Step 5

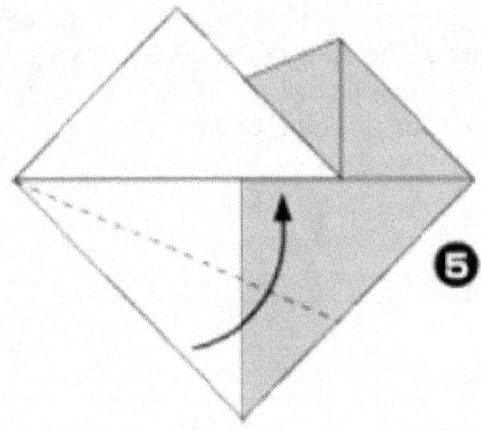

Repeat step four on the lower left side, as shown, by folding the lower corner up to the center, following the dotted line. This will be forming a second "flap". Both flaps together now form a square.

Step 6

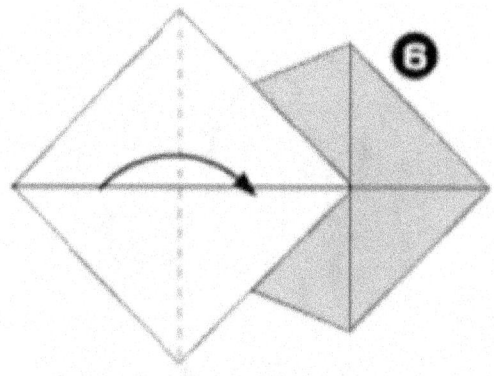

Now fold the left point of the square formed by the flaps over to meet the other point of the square.

Step 7

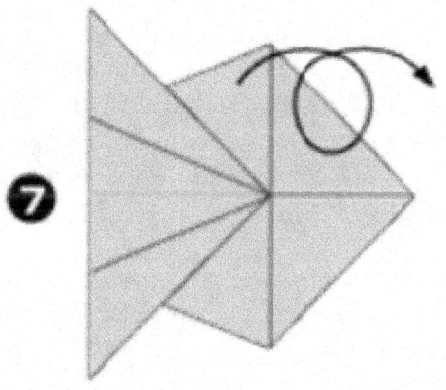

Turn the entire piece over.

Step 8

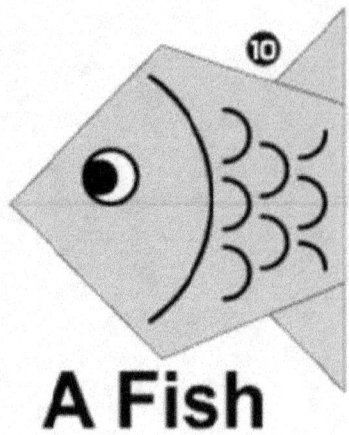

A Fish

Ta-da! All done! You've made you're first origami fish! Now you can customize your fish to your liking. Maybe you can even make it some fish friends!

Fun fact: Fish have been around for more than 450 million years, even before the dinosaurs!

Did you know… The first book about origami was published in 1797. It was called 'Sembazuru Orikata' (Thousand Crane Folding), and it was written by Akisato Rito. Instead of paper folding instructions, the book talked about different cultural customs and traditions in Japan.

Chapter 10: Owl

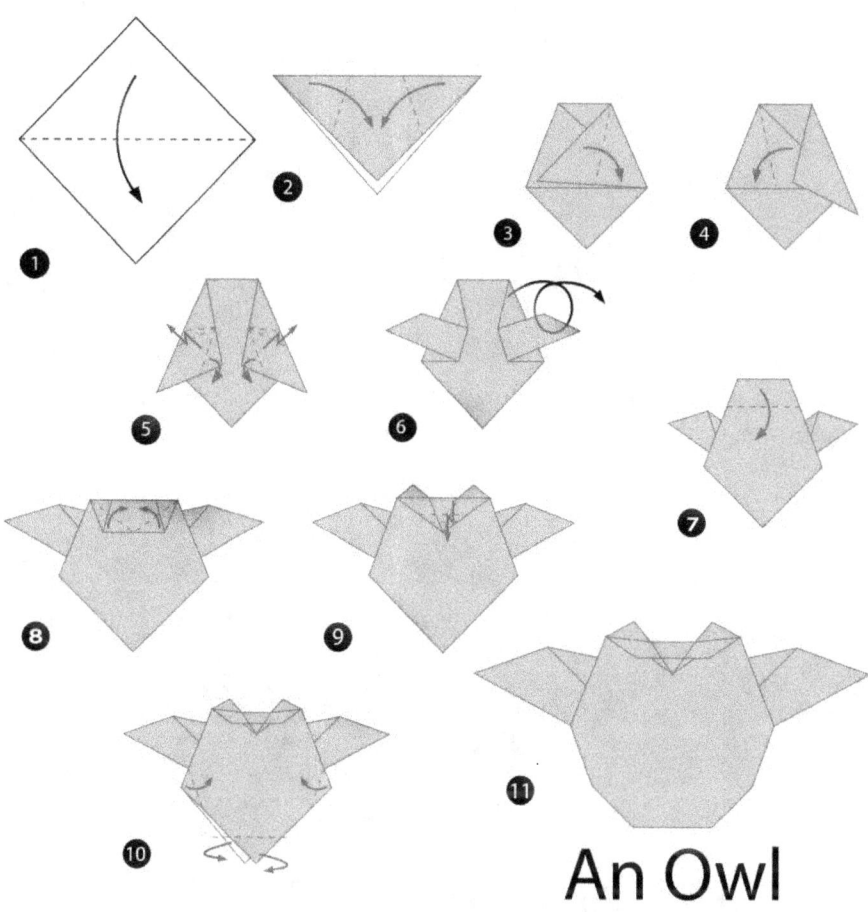

An Owl

Start with your paper flat on the surface, color (or pattern) side down, laying in the shape of a diamond. Just like our other animals, the color or pattern facing down will soon become the color of your owl's "feathers."

Step 1

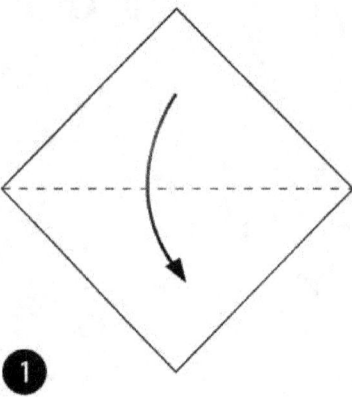

Fold your paper in half from the top to the bottom, as shown by the dotted line.

Step 2

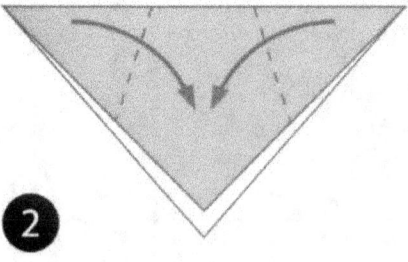

See the dotted lines and the arrows? Fold the left corner across so the tip touches the opposite edge, as shown in the picture below. Then do the same with the right corner, so they overlap in the center. Remember to crease well.

Step 3

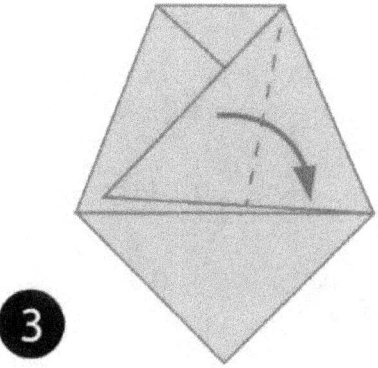

Fold back along the dotted line following the direction of the arrow, as shown in the picture. You can see what it should look like in step 4.

Step 4:

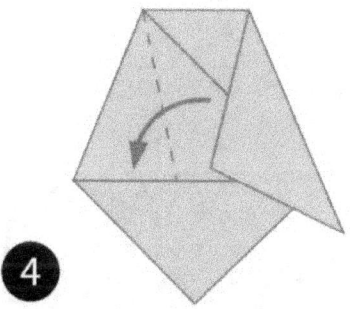

Just like in step three, fold the flap that's resting beneath the side you just folded by following the dotted lines again. These are your Owl's wings.

Step 5

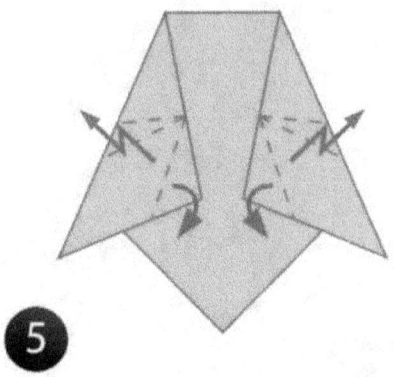

Now we need to finish the wings. Take a look at the dotted lines that are more towards the center of your piece, along with the two arrows in the center. Fold each point backwards and beneath the rest of the flaps. Crease well. Now see the remaining dotted lines with the zig-zag arrows on each side? Perform a stair fold on the left flap, and then repeat on the right side. You can look at the picture in step 6 to see what it should look like.

Step 6

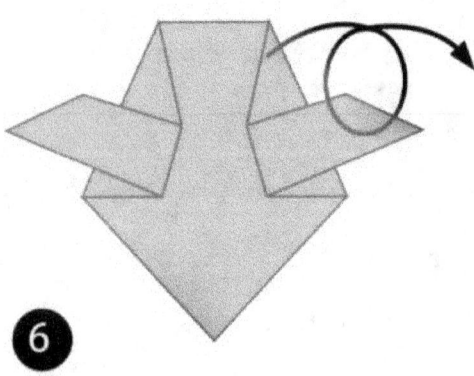

Ok, this isn't really a fold! Just turn the whole origami piece over. Super easy!

Step 7

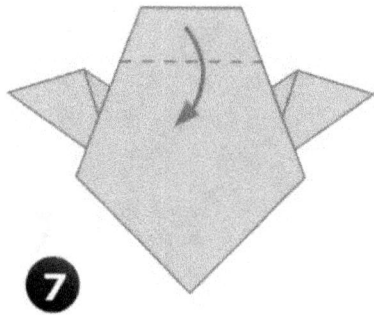

Fold the top down, as shown with the dotted line and arrow. Crease well here, we're making the owl's face!

Step 8

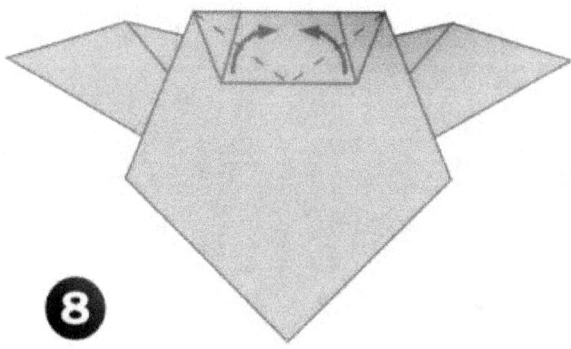

Follow the dotted lines on the left and fold the corner up so that it touches the top edge. Repeat this for the right side. Crease well.

Step 9

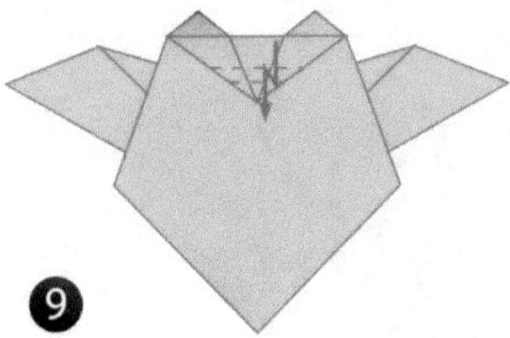

This might look a little tricky because it's on a small point, but it's really not. This is just a stair fold. Remember you can always refer back to the folds section towards the beginning of the book if you need to refresh your memory.

Step 10

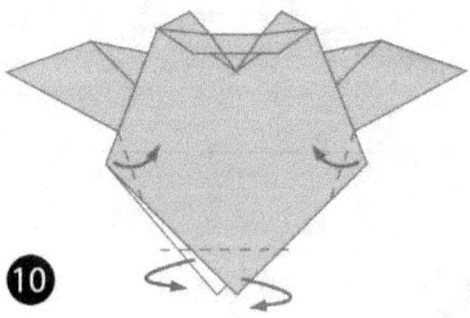

See the arrows at each corner on the side? Fold these two corners backwards along the dotted lines and crease well. Now, see how there are two layers of paper at the bottom? Fold the top layer backwards so that it's folded to the inside. Then fold the remaining bottom layer upward so that it's on the inside as well.

Step 11

An Owl

Ta-da! Your owl is now complete! You can add some texture lines in for feathers, or leave it as-is. Draw on some facial features, and decorate your owl however you like. Just have a hoot!

Fun fact: There are no owls in Antarctica! It's too cold, even for them. Can you think of some animals that *do* live in Antarctica? Are there any in this book?

Did you know... The Guinness Book of World Records has dozens of records regarding the craft of origami, like the object that has been made with the most folds, the smallest and the biggest objects, fastest time for folding 100 cranes, and more.

Chapter 11: Bat

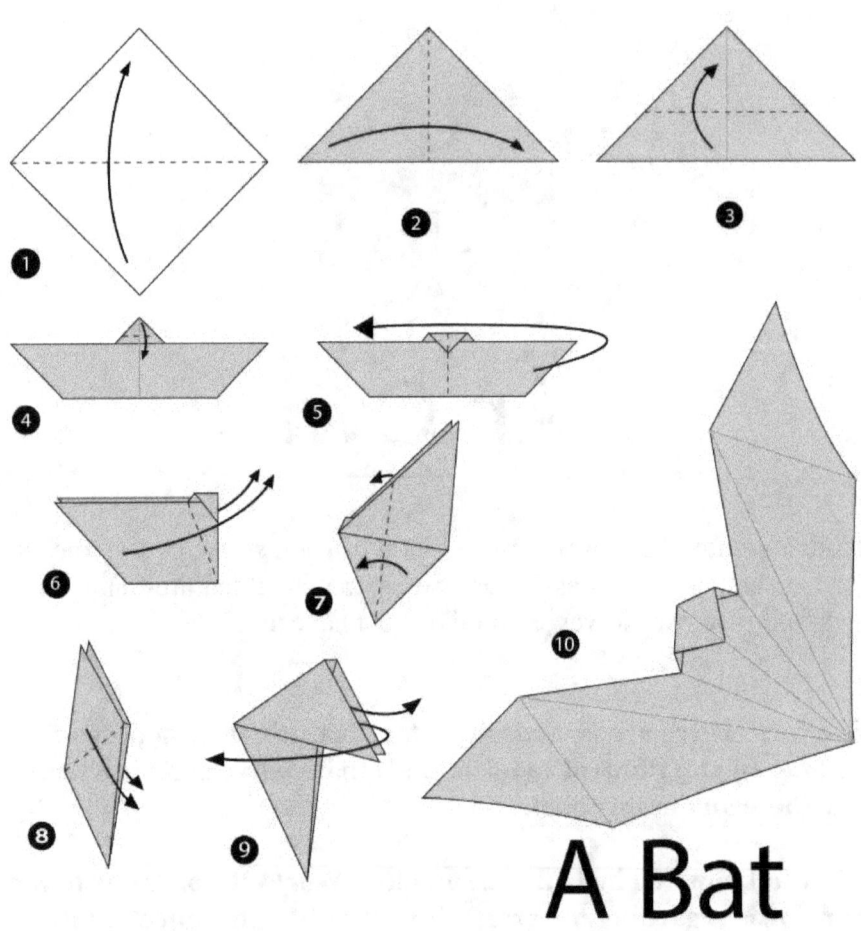

A Bat

Start with your square sheet of paper flat on your work surface with the color (or pattern) side facing down (this will be the outside, or "fur" color of your bat). Lay it down this way in the shape of a diamond (remember you can follow the picture instructions as well).

Step 1

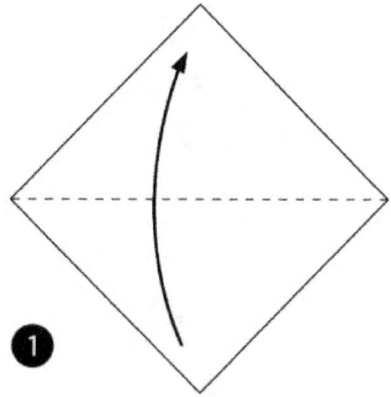

Fold your paper in half from the bottom corner to the top corner. You will now have a triangle.

Step 2

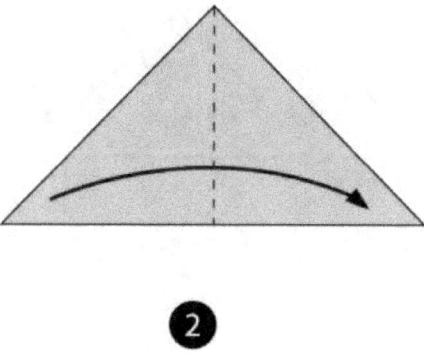

Fold the left triangle corner over to meet the right corner (in half from left to right). Crease well, and then unfold this so it is back to a triangle.

Step 3

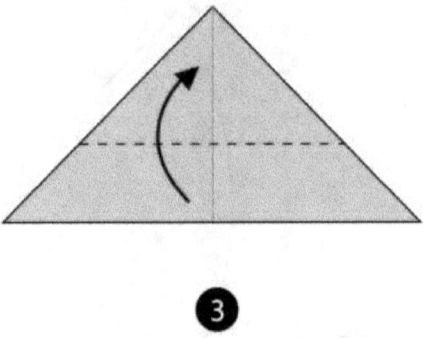

Fold the bottom half of the triangle up, leaving a bit of the top point of the triangle peeking out (take a peek at the picture to see what I mean). Crease well.

Step 4

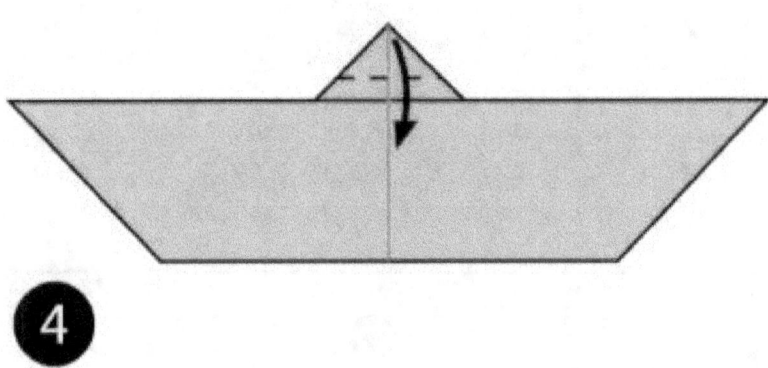

Fold down the top point you left peeking out in half from the top to bottom so that it overlaps the other piece you just folded (see the picture below). This is going to be your bat's cute little face!

Step 5

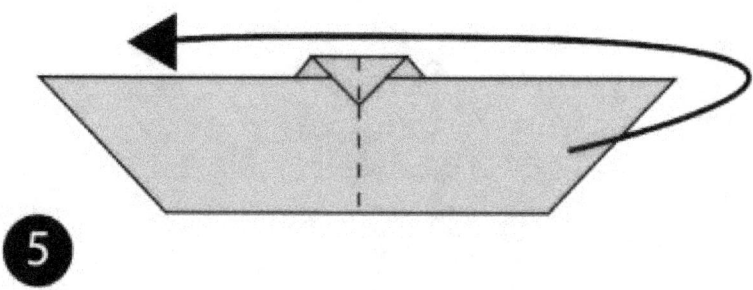

Fold in half from the right remaining corner back to the left. Crease well.

Step 6

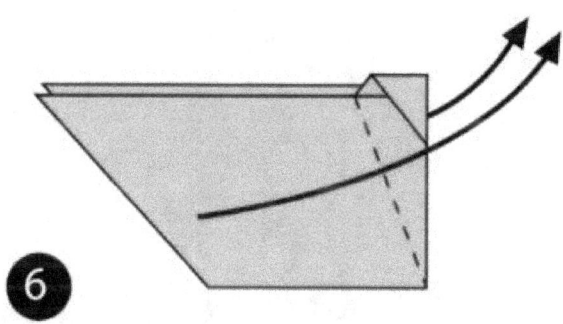

Fold the top wing over and up a bit (follow the dotted line). Repeat this on the other side to the other wing.

Step 7

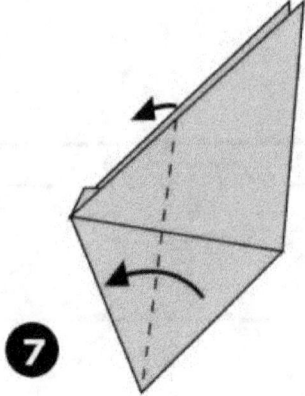

Fold in half, taking the right side over to the left (again, follow the dotted line in the picture)

Step 8

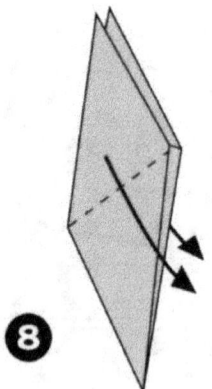

Fold down the top point in half. Repeat this fold for the top point on the other side.

Step 9

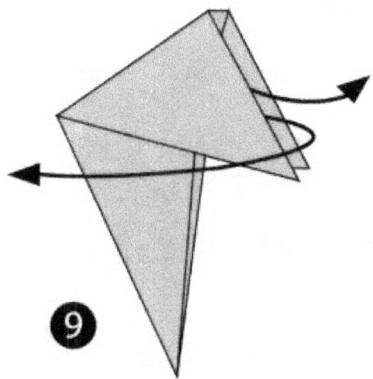

See the arrows in the picture? Pull each side as shown in each direction of the arrows.

Step 10

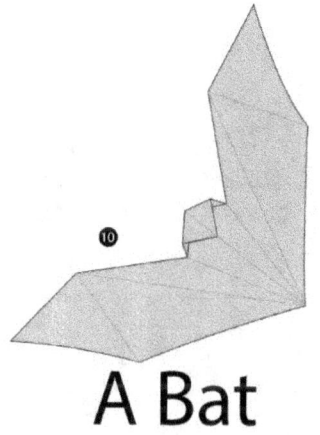

A Bat

Flatten things out, and take a look! You're done! You can decorate your bat, draw on a face and other details, or leave it as is.

Fun fact: There are over 1000 different varieties of bats. Which does your origami bat look like most?

Did you know… before "origami", the practice of paper folding was called "orikata" which means "folded shape".

Chapter 12: Bear Cub

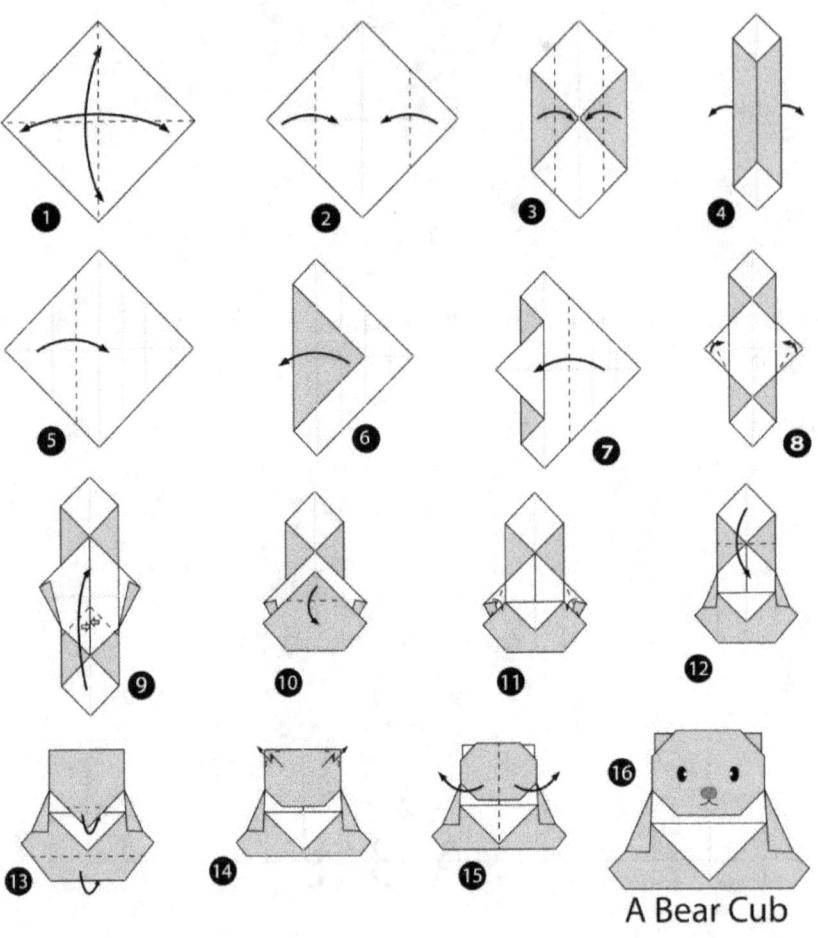

A Bear Cub

Start with your paper flat on your surface, color (or pattern) side face down, in the shape of a diamond. The colored side will be the outside of your cute little bear cub.

Step 1

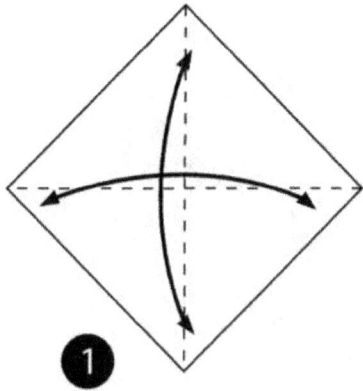

Fold in half from the left corner to the right, unfold. Now fold in half from top to bottom, and unfold. You'll have another cross in the center like many of our other projects.

Step 2

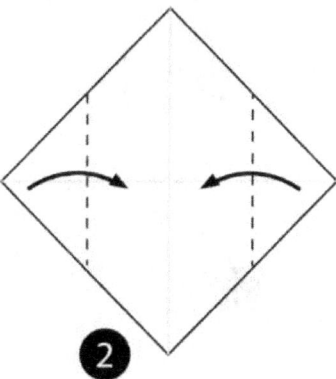

Fold the left and right corners to meet in the middle on the center crease, as shown in the picture.

Step 3

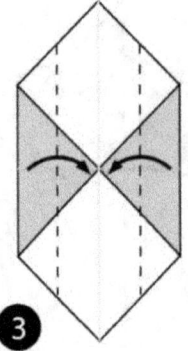

Fold the left edge to the center crease, and repeat for the right edge.

Step 4

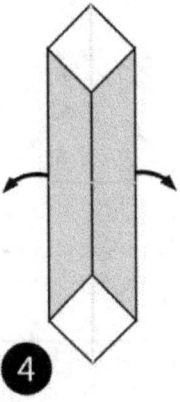

Unfold all of the folds you've made so far. I know it seems odd, but trust me!

Step 5

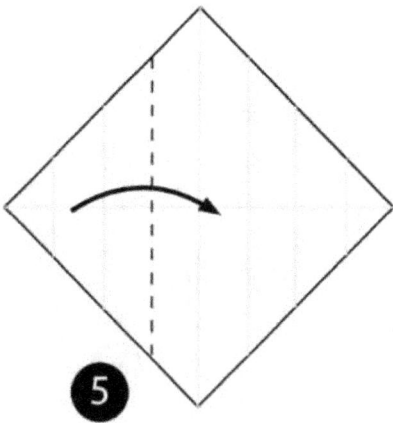

See all of the creases you've made? There are eight all together. Now, fold the left corner along the dotted line as shown, so that the point rests on the sixth crease counting from the left.

Step 6

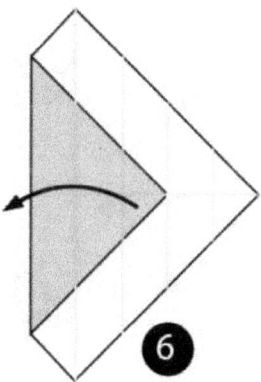

Fold the top flap to the left along the very middle crease as shown in the picture.

Step 7

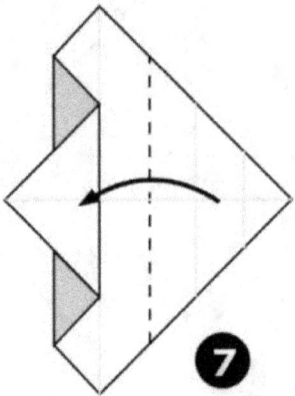

Repeat steps 5, 6, and 7 on the right side to match the left.

Step 8

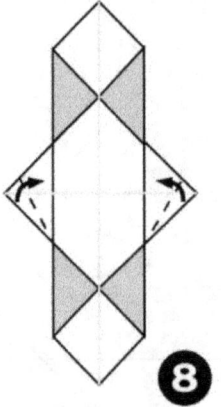

See the dotted lines? Fold each corner along the dotted lines shown.

Step 9

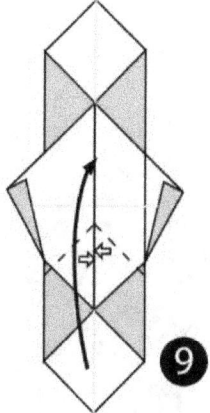

See the white arrows? Yes, it's another squash fold! You're getting good at this by now! Open up the pockets slightly where the white arrows are located and as you fold over the very bottom corner upwards, the pockets should open up at the same time and then flatten them as you complete the fold. See picture below for confirmation.

Step 10

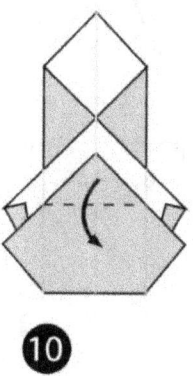

Follow the arrow, folding down along the dotted line.

Step 11

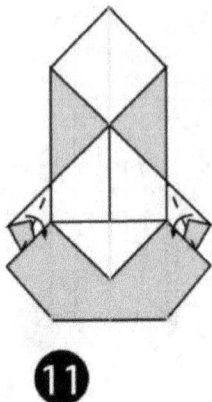

Lift the left side open a bit and fold inward and over, as shown in the picture. Repeat on the right side. These will make the bears little arms.

Step 12

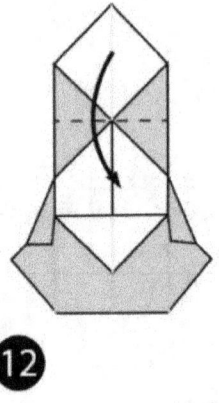

Fold the top point down along the dotted line. See picture below for confirmation.

Step 13

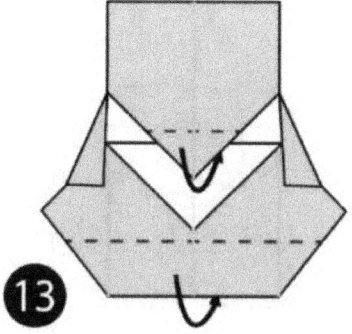

See the dotted line at the top? Fold backwards along the dotted line, tucking under. Fold backwards along the lower dotted line as well.

Step 14

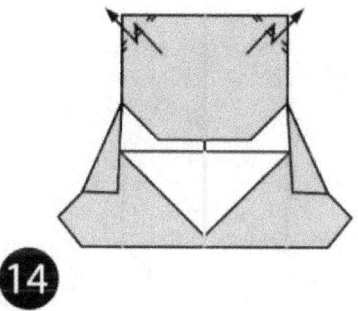

Lift the left edge up a bit and fold inward along the dotted line but still leaving out the tip. This is sometimes called a step fold because it forms a "step" like a staircase; check the "folds" chapter if you need to. Repeat this on the right side.

Step 15

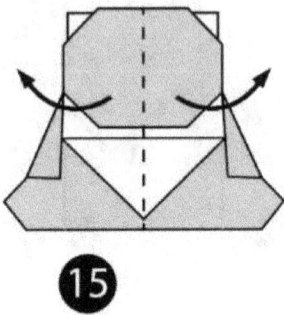

Fold the entire piece in half making a crease in the middle, then unfold it again.

Step 16

A Bear Cub

Draw on your bear cub's face, and you're ready to tame! Give your bear a pretty necklace or a bow tie (maybe this cub is fancy!) and let him join your other animal friends.

Fun Fact: Bears have an extremely good sense of smell, better than dogs, and maybe even better than any other animal!

Did you know… the origami crane has become an international symbol for peace. An organization called "Wings for Peace" made the world's largest paper crane in 1999. It was 1,750 pounds and 215 feet tall.

Chapter 13: Lion

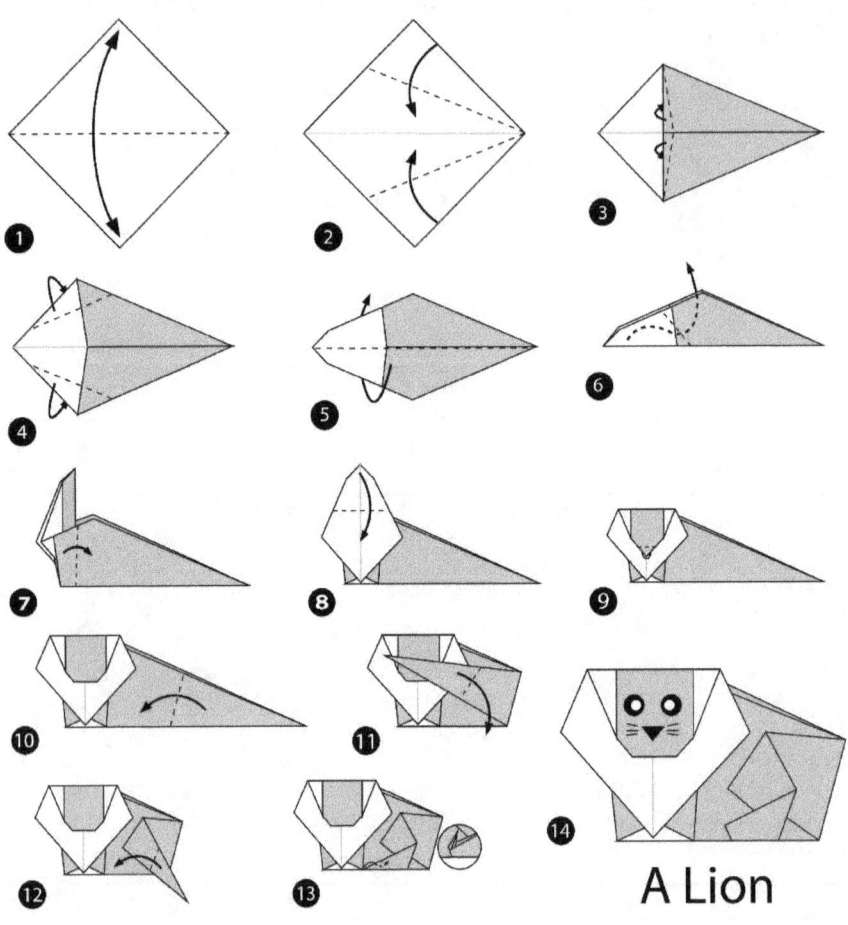

A Lion

Real tigers and lions don't really get along, but this paper lion can be your paper tiger's best friend! Start with your paper flat on your work surface in the shape of a diamond, with the color (or pattern) side down. This color will soon be the "fur" color of your lion.

Step 1

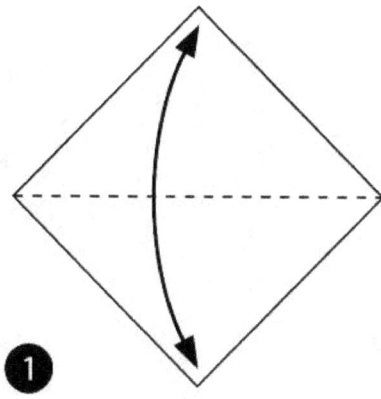

Fold the top corner down to the bottom, as shown in the picture, then unfold again.

Step 2

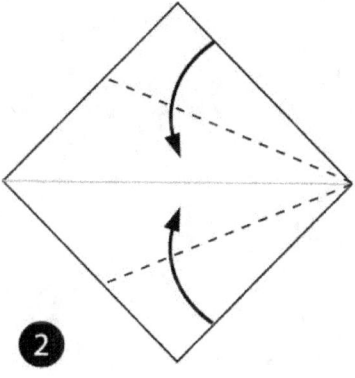

See the dotted lines? Fold along them so that the edges meet at the center crease.

Step 3

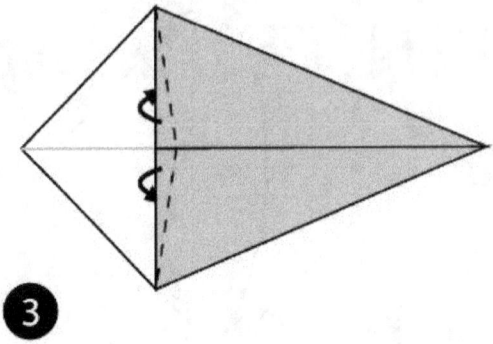

Fold along the dotted lines, but folding backwards tucking in.

Step 4

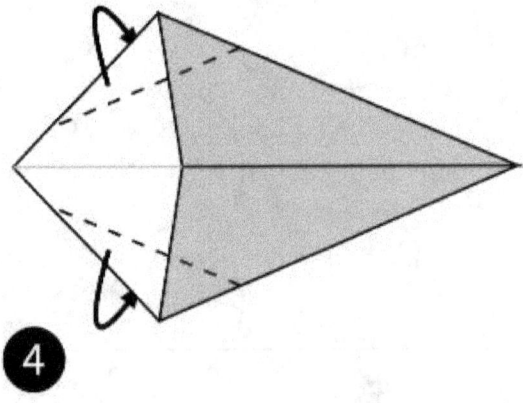

See the dotted lines? Fold backwards along them.

Step 5

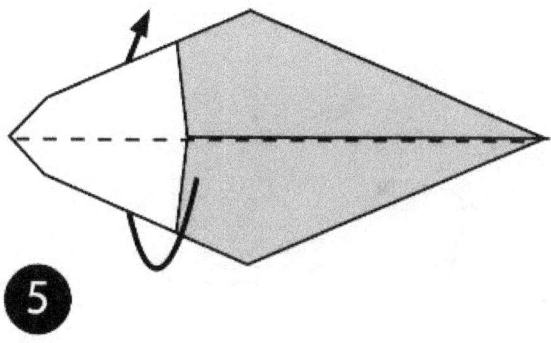

Fold in half as shown, by folding the bottom half under.

Step 6

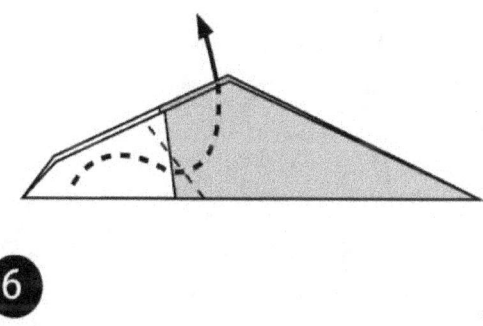

Fold upward and inward, pushing in, as shown in the picture (this is the squash fold again).

Step 7

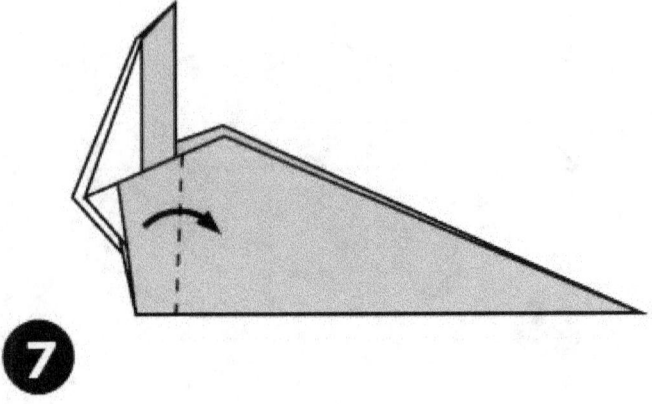

Fold the top flap along the dotted line as shown.

Step 8

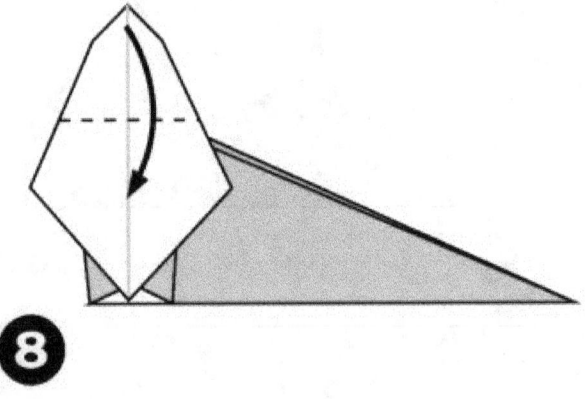

Fold down on the dotted line like you see in the picture.

Step 9

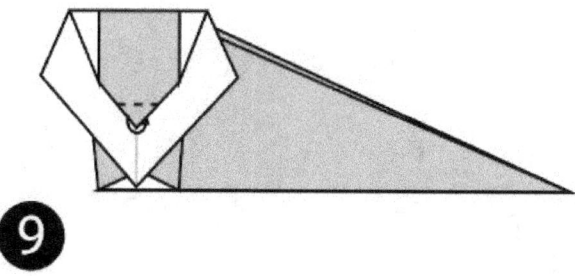

See the dotted line? Fold the little point backwards, tucking in as shown in the picture.

Step 10

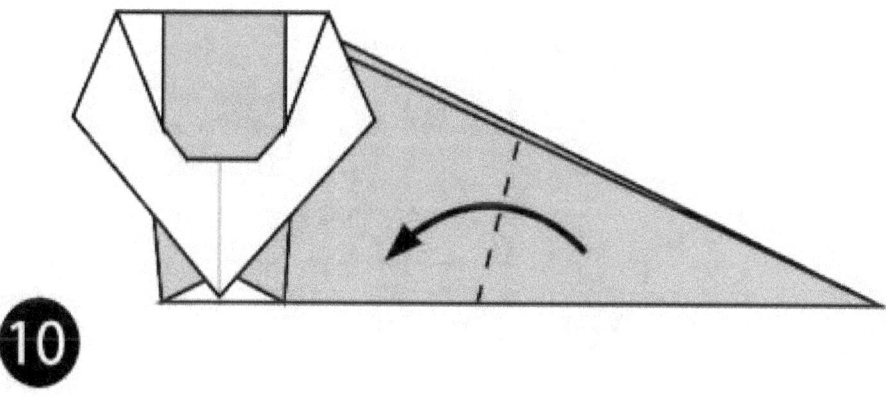

Following the dotted line, fold the point over from the right towards the left.

Step 11

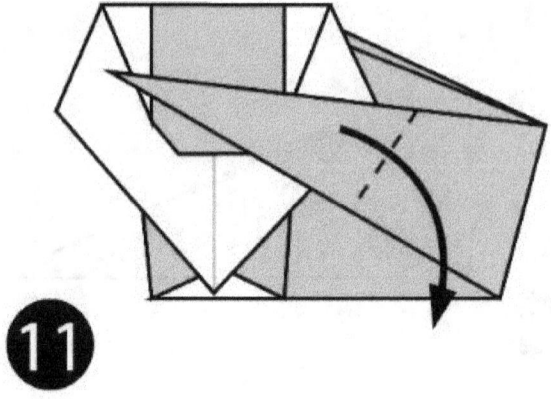

Follow the dotted line again, folding the point down and back towards the right.

Step 12

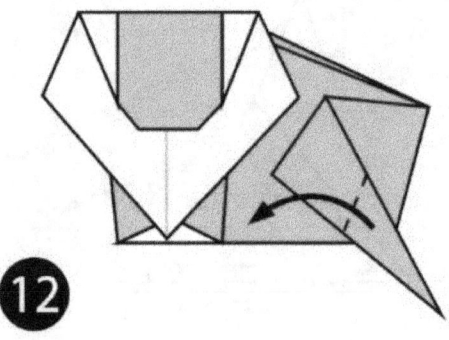

One more time, fold the tip back up and to the left so that it lines up along the bottom edge.

Step 13

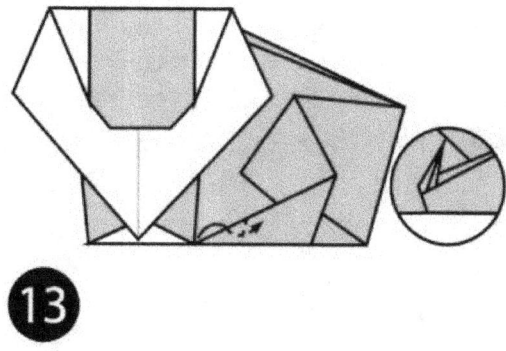

Fold the very tip inward, tucking it in.

Step 14

A Lion

Congratulations! Draw on your lion's face, decorate his mane, and give him a name!

Fun Fact: Both male and female lions can roar. Their roar can be heard up to five miles away!

Did you know… origami has become such a popular form of art that there are now several origami associations that have been formed all over the world. There is the Origami Center of America and the British Origami Society, among others. Most major cities now have "origami masters".

Chapter 14: Penguin

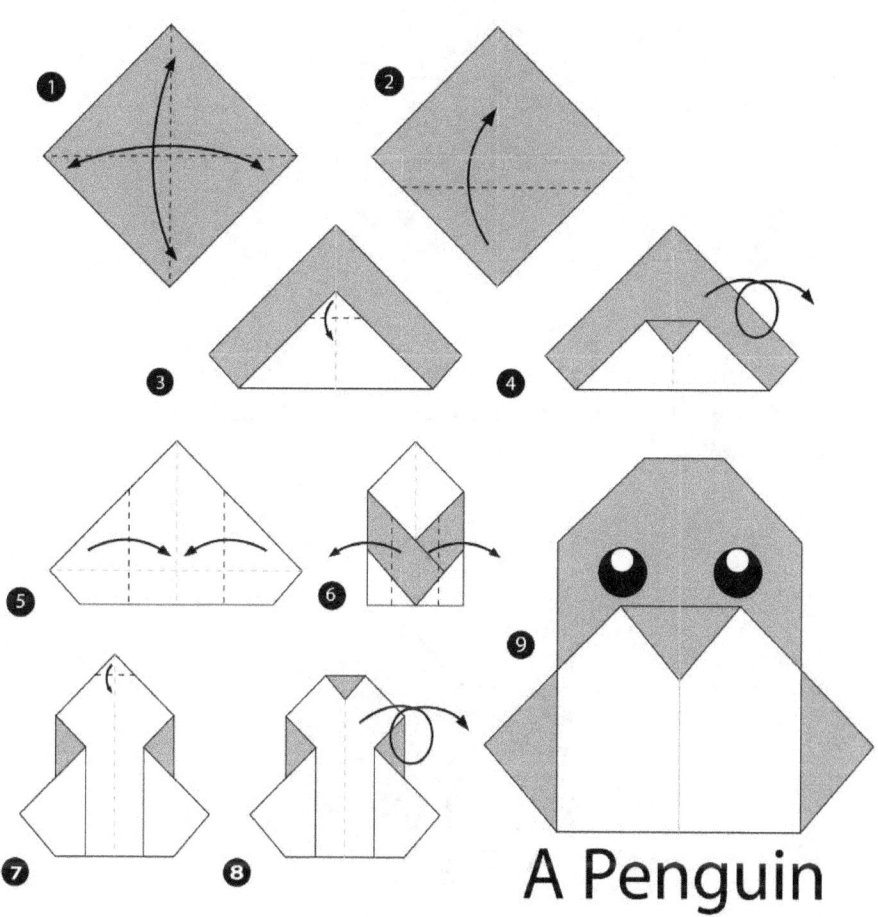

A Penguin

Were penguins one of the animals you guessed that live in Antarctica? This paper one doesn't have to live in cold weather, though. Maybe this penguin is a tropical penguin! Start with your paper flat on your work surface with the color (or pattern) side facing up. Lay your paper out so that it is in the shape of a diamond.

Step 1

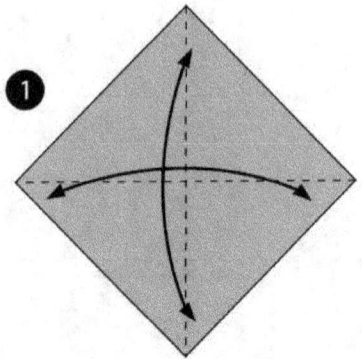

Fold the left corner over to the right, folding in half, then unfold it again. Repeat this with the bottom corned folded up to the top. Unfold once again.

Step 2

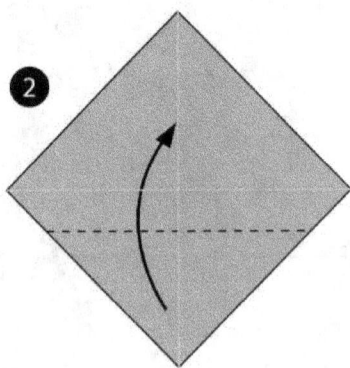

Following the dotted line, fold the lower corner up, creasing where you see the dotted line in the picture.

Step 3

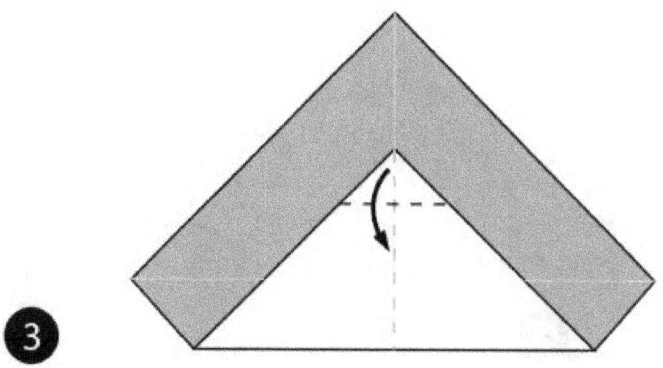

Following the dotted line, fold the top point down as shown.

Step 4

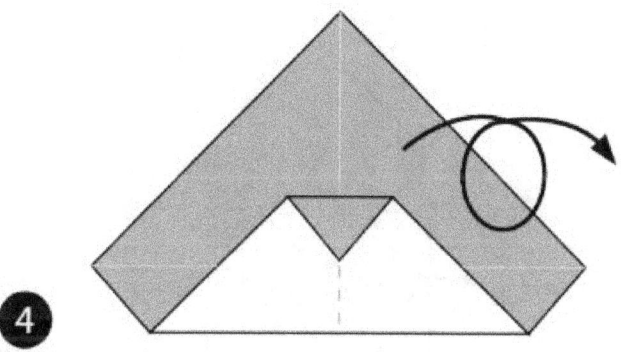

Turn the whole piece over.

Step 5

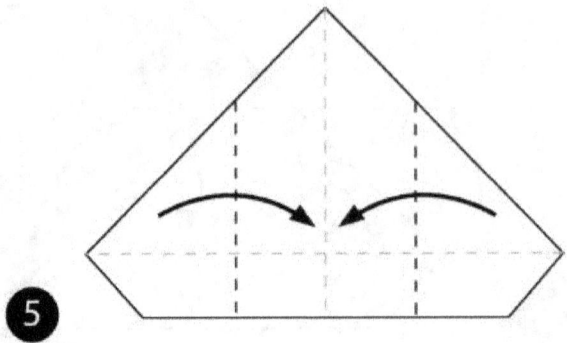

Fold the left corner a bit past the center line, as shown. Then fold the right in the same way. The two will overlap a little in the middle.

Step 6

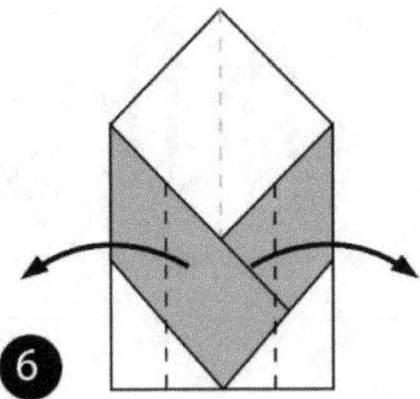

Follow the arrows and fold along the dotted lines, doing the left side first, then the right.

Step 7

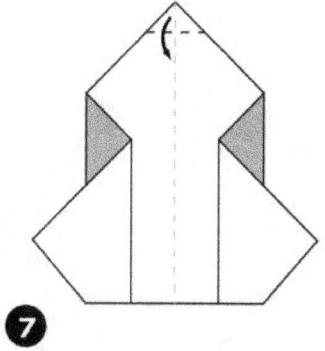

Fold the top point down, as shown.

Step 8

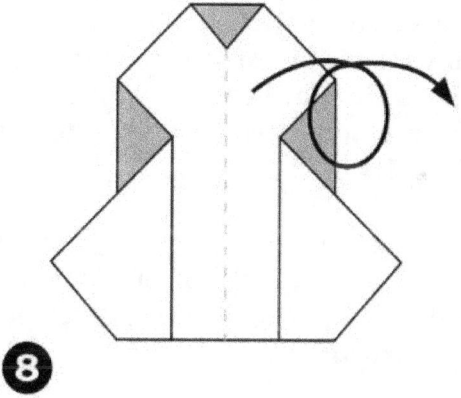

Turn the whole piece over.

Step 9

A Penguin

Woo! You're done! Draw on eyes, color the beak, and maybe give your penguin a scarf to keep him warm. Unless your penguin really is tropical, then maybe give him a swim suit and a cold drink!

Fun Fact: There are many varieties of penguins. For example, Emperor Penguins are the tallest species, standing about 4 feet tall. The smallest is the Little Blue Penguin, which is only roughly 16 inches. The fastest penguin species is the Gentoo Penguin, which can swim up to 22 miles per hour.

Did you know… Akira Yoshizawa is often considered the Grand Master of origami. He created over 50,000 origami models. He also invented a method called wet-folding and developed a method of drawing origami instructions.

Chapter 15: Platypus

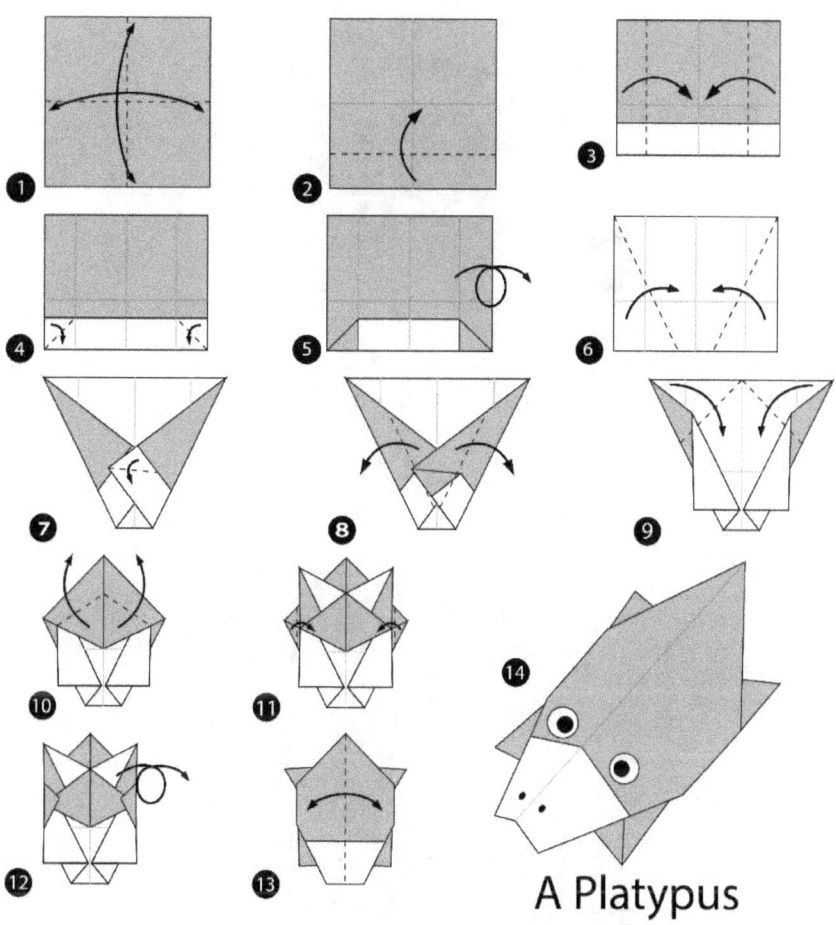

A Platypus

Have you ever heard of a platypus? It's a very unique creature! For this animal, instead of putting your paper color side down, place it flat on your work surface in the shape of a square with the color side facing up.

Step 1

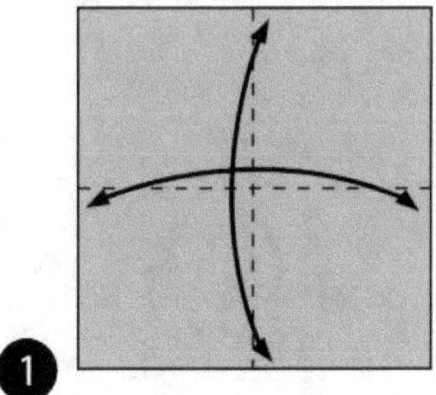

Fold the top edge to the bottom edge, and unfold it again. Repeat this with the left edge to the right edge, and unfold again.

Step 2

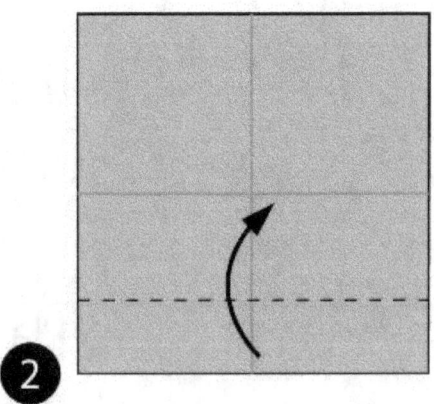

Following the dotted line, fold upward almost to the center crease, but not quite.

Step 3

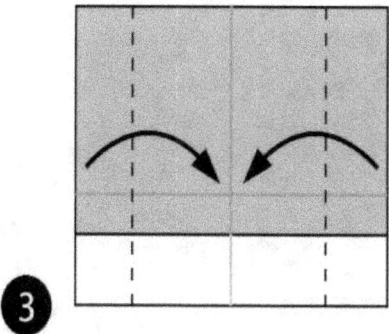

Fold both the left edge, and then the right edge, in to the center crease so that they meet, then unfold again.

Step 4

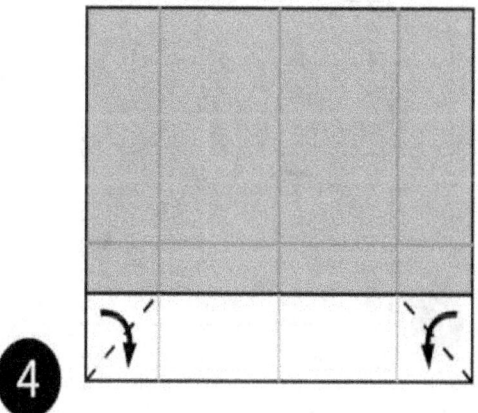

Following the dotted lines, fold both the left and right corners down to the bottom edge as shown.

Step 5

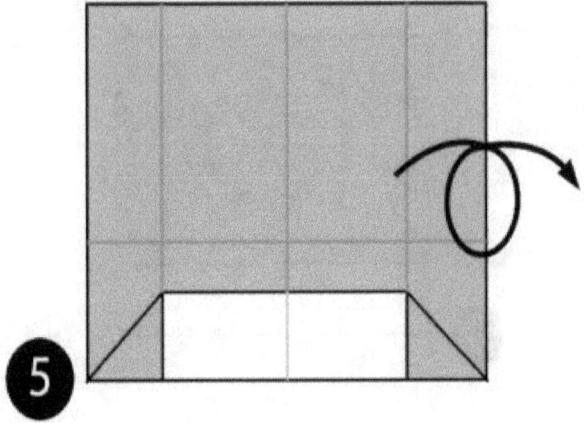

Turn the whole piece over.

Step 6

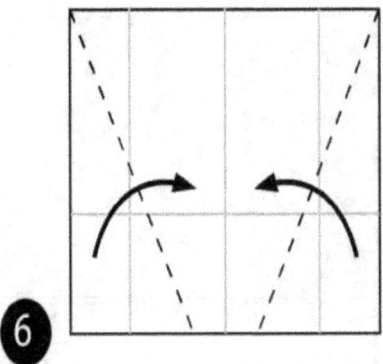

Following the dotted lines, fold the left side over, and then the right side. The right side will overlap the left, as shown on the next step.

Step 7

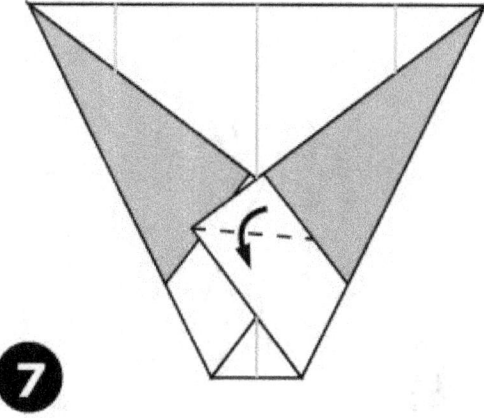

See the dotted line and the arrow? Following the arrow, fold down the corner along the dotted line.

Step 8

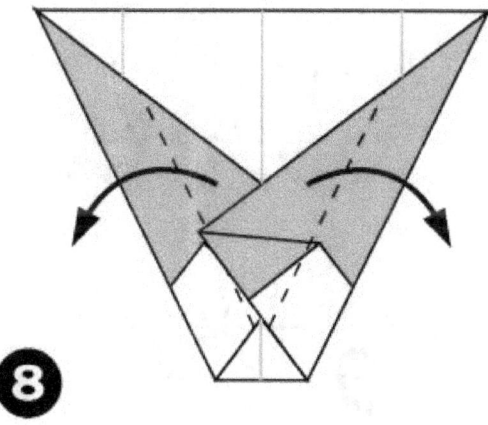

Follow the dotted lines and fold the right side first (the part on top) and then the left.

Step 9

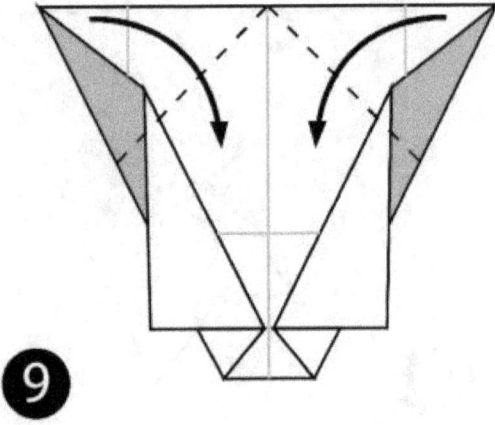

Fold the top two corners down in order to meet the center crease, as shown.

Step 10

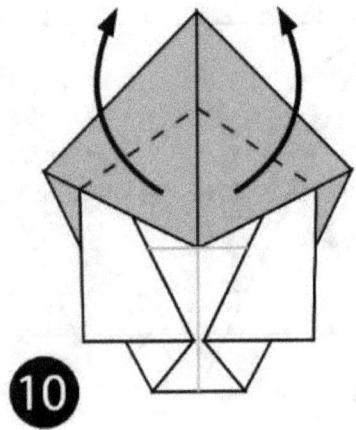

Following the dotted lines, fold up and outward a bit for both sides, as shown.

Step 11

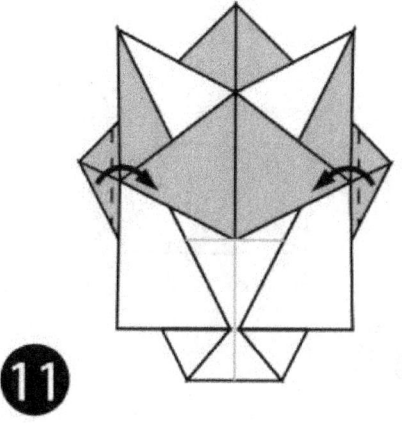

Fold the left and right "tabs" over as shown.

Step 12

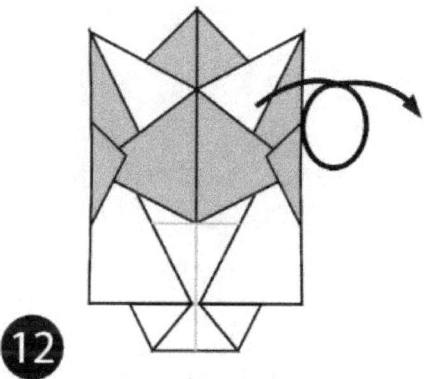

Turn the whole piece over.

Step 13

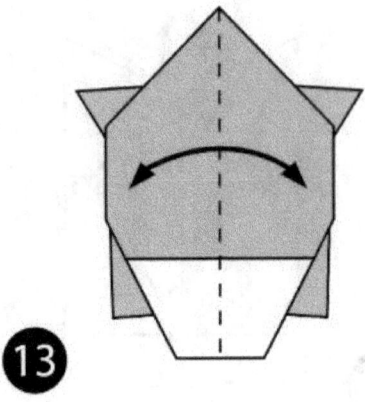

Fold in half with a mountain fold as shown and crease, then unfold.

Step 14

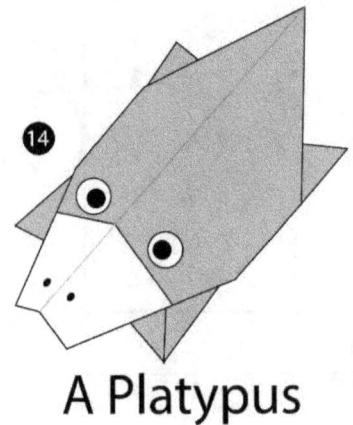

A Platypus

Draw eyes and other details to spruce up your new friend! Maybe give him some cool sunglasses?

Fun Fact: When the platypus was first brought from Australia to Britain, people didn't believe that it was a real animal because of its strange appearance. It has a paddle-like tail like a beaver, a furry body much like an otter, and webbed feet and a bill like a duck.

Did you know… the world record for longest origami snake is 152.52625 feet long. This world record was made on March 11th 2001 in Singapore. There is also a record for the longest caterpillar, which is 2,128 feet. It was made in Germany in October of 2004 by 60 men with 25,000 sheets of paper.

Chapter 16: Gorilla

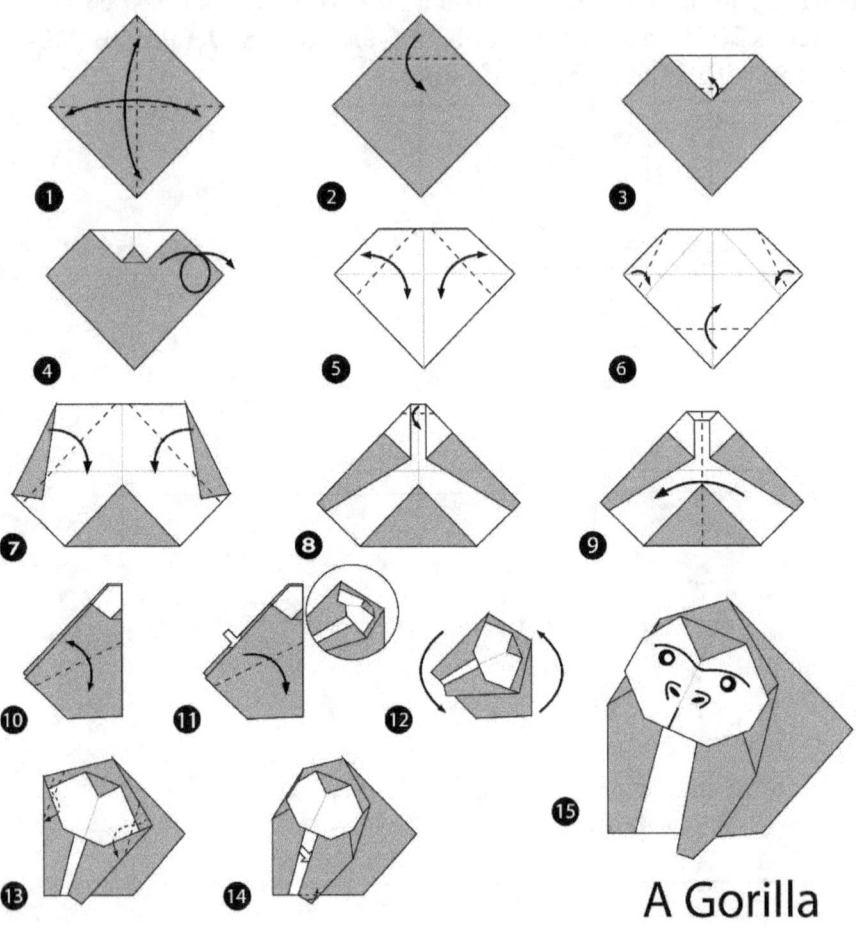

A Gorilla

We've got felines, canines, fish, bears, birds… now we need a primate! Start this project with the paper flat on your work surface, color (or pattern) side facing up again this time, placed down in the shape of a diamond.

Step 1

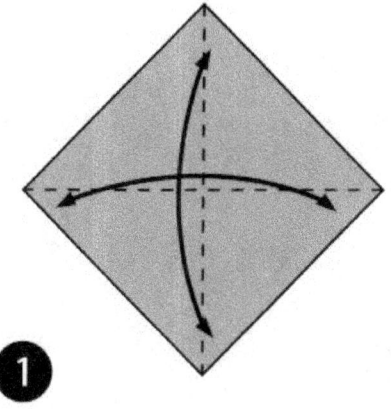

Fold the left corner over to the right, crease well and then unfold again. Next, fold the top corner down to the bottom, crease, and unfold as well.

Step 2

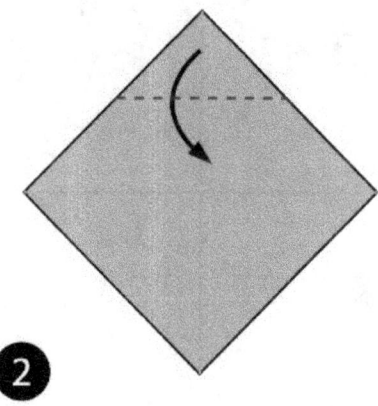

Fold the top point down to the center as shown in the picture.

Step 3

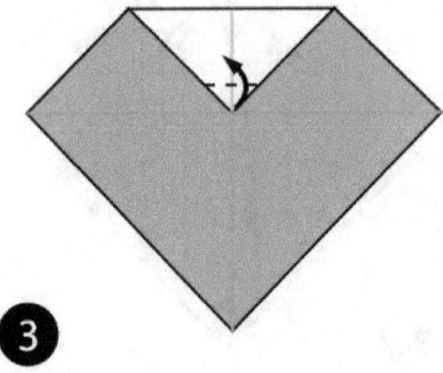

See the little dotted line and arrow? Fold the little point up, as shown.

Step 4

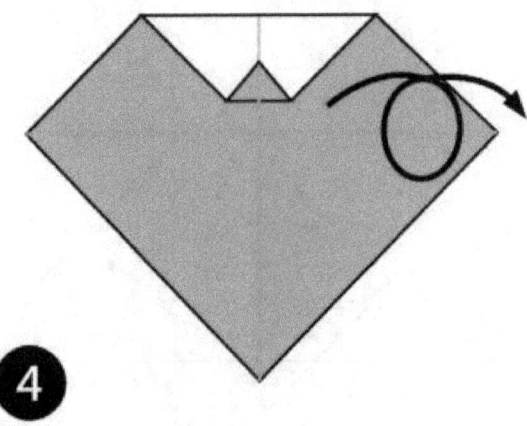

You probably remember what this symbol means, and it's super easy! Just turn the whole piece over.

Step 5

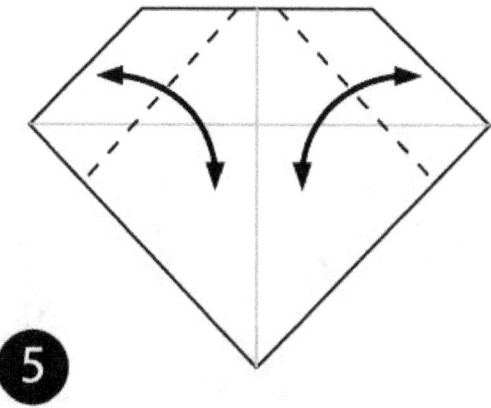

Take a look at the dotted lines and arrows on both sides. Fold along the dotted lines in the direction of the arrows as show. Remember to crease well, then unfold.

Step 6

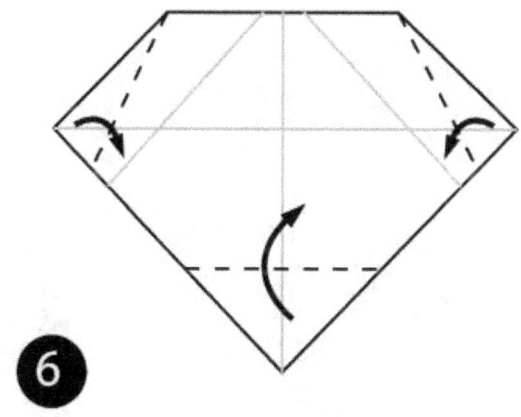

Here you have 3 folds to make, but don't worry, it's pretty easy. Fold the left corner over so that the tip of it goes just a little past the crease you made on the left in step 5. Now do the same thing with the right side. Finally, fold the bottom corner up as shown in the picture by the dotted line.

Step 7

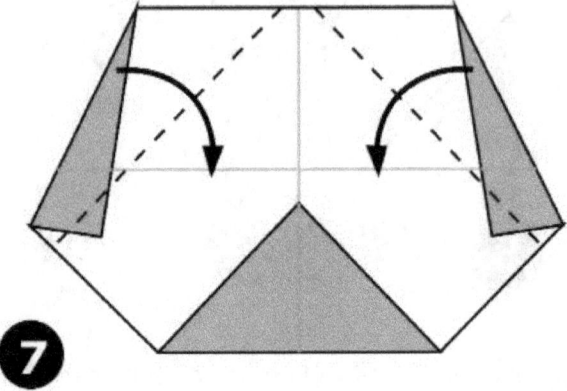

Fold along the dotted line on the left in the direction of the arrow as shown. Do the same thing following the dotted line on the right side.

Step 8

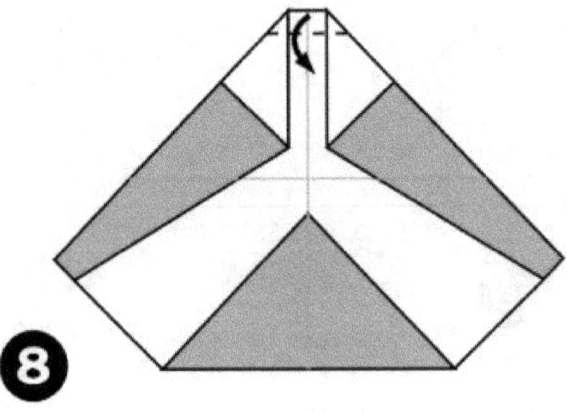

See the little dotted line at the top again? Fold down along the dotted line as shown in the picture.

Step 9

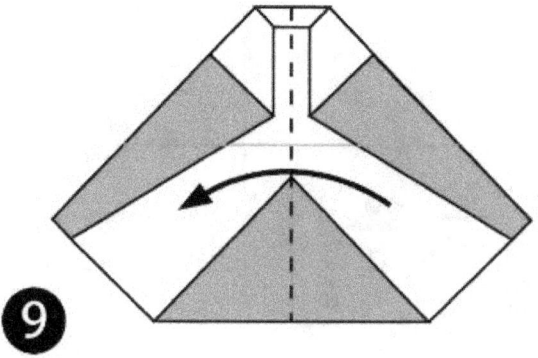

Fold the right half over to the left, so that the project is folded in half.

Step 10

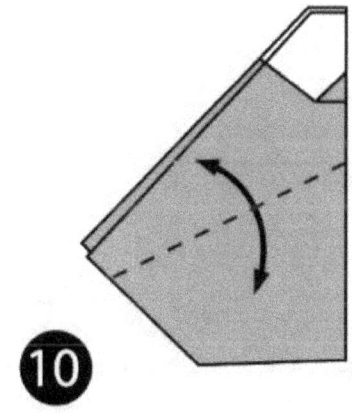

Fold along the dotted line downwards as shown in the picture. Crease well, and then unfold. Repeat these steps again but folding along the dotted lines backwards.

Step 11

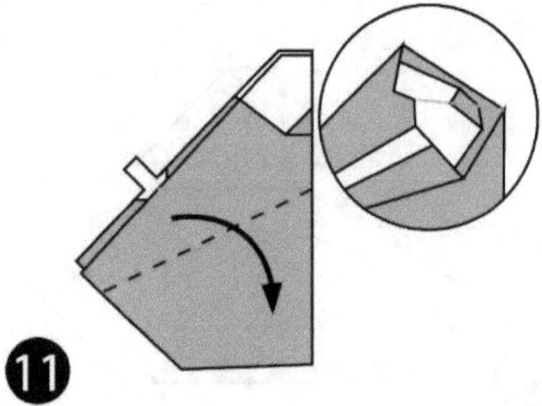

See where the white arrow is? Lift this up a bit so it starts to open and then do a squash fold along the dotted line as shown. You can see what it should look like in step 12.

Step 12

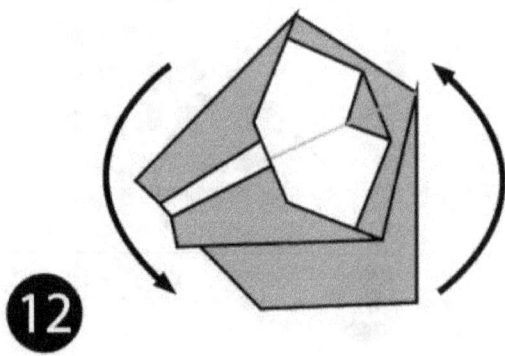

Rotate your origami project to the left, as shown by the arrows. You can see what I mean and how it should look in step 13.

Step 13

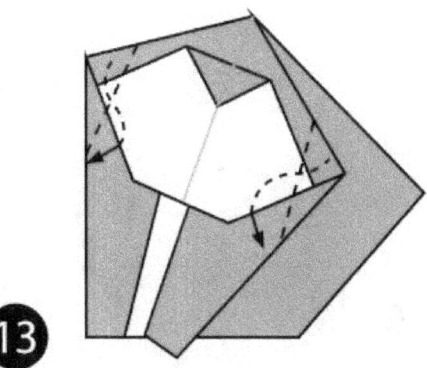

See the arrows and dotted lines on both sides? Do a pocket fold, tucking the points inside. Remember to do this on both sides, as shown in the picture. You're almost done!

Step 14

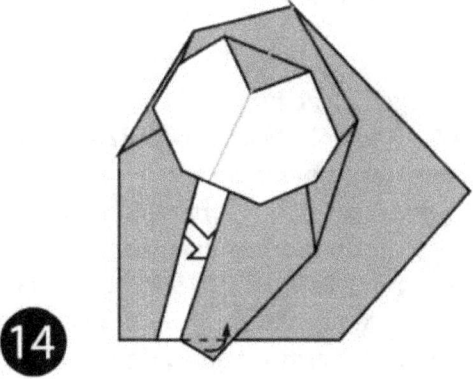

See the white arrow and dotted line? Lift up the side that the white arrow points to, and do a pocket fold where the dotted line is shown, tucking inside.

Step 15

A Gorilla

Boom! Your gorilla just needs some eyes, nose, and other details you might want to add, and then he (or she) is done!

Fun Fact: After chimpanzees and bonobos, gorillas are the closest living relatives to humans. They share about 95% of their DNA with people, and our two species come from the same common ancestor.

Did you know... Alongside the largest origami projects, there are also world records for the smallest pieces. Professor Watanabe in Japan folded the smallest paper crane; it's just 1mm in size and was made by using tweezers and a microscope. A Frenchmen named Eric Roudiere made the smallest origami chicken at just 1.5 mm x 1.5 mm x 1.19 mm. March 16th 1995, a kid named Christian Thorp Frederiksen who was just 12 years of age made the smallest paper aircraft, which is 2.5 mm x 1 mm, and a man named Christian Elbrandt folded a 2.7 mm origami frog that can jump to 103mm.

Chapter 17: Swan

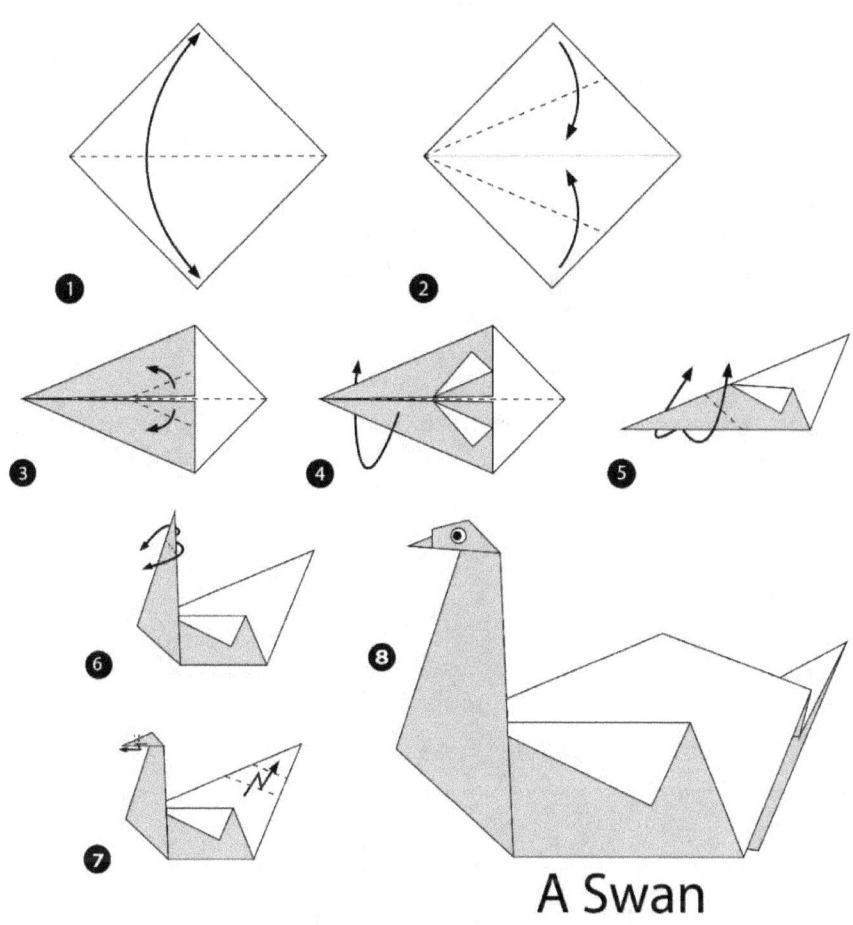

A Swan

We have a penguin (they swim in the water), so maybe it needs another feathered water friend. Start with your paper flat on your work surface, color (or pattern) side down, in the shape of a diamond. This color facing down will be the outside, or "feathers", of your swan.

Step 1

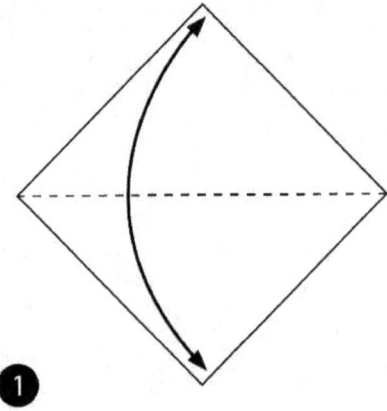

Fold the bottom point up to meet the top point, making a center crease. Unfold again.

Step 2

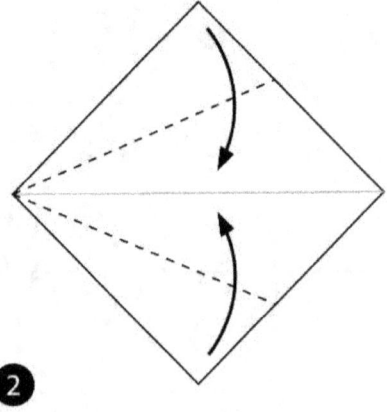

See the dotted lines? Fold each edge along the dotted lines meeting the middle crease as shown.

Step 3

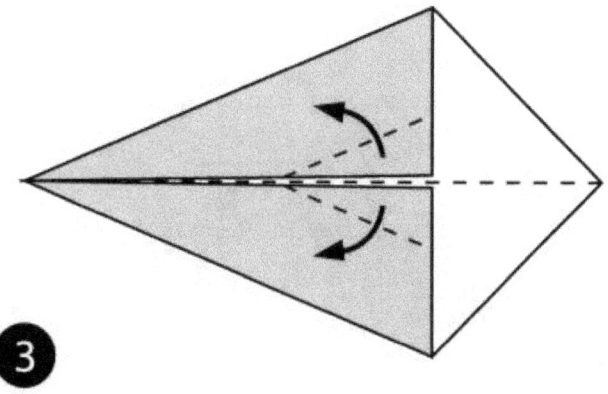

Fold the inner corners out along the dotted lines.

Step 4

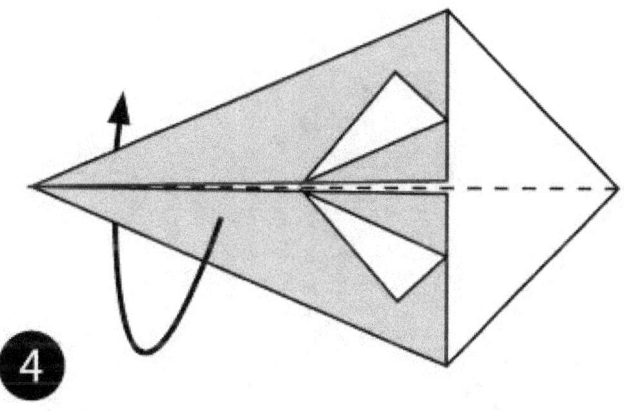

Fold the whole piece in half with a mountain fold by folding the two sides together.

Step 5

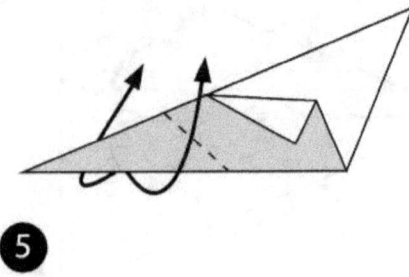

See the arrows? Lift the point upward, following the arrows, and fold in the center, tucking, with a pocket fold.

Step 6

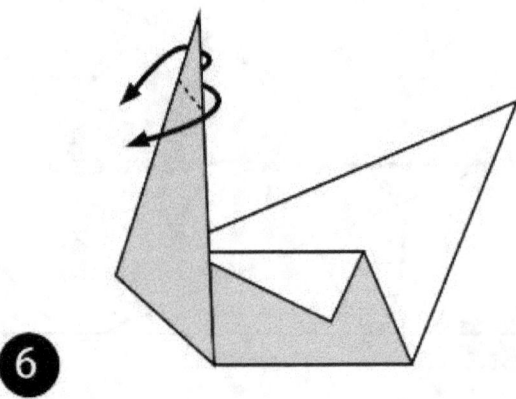

Repeat the technique you used in step five on the very tip here, as shown.

Step 7

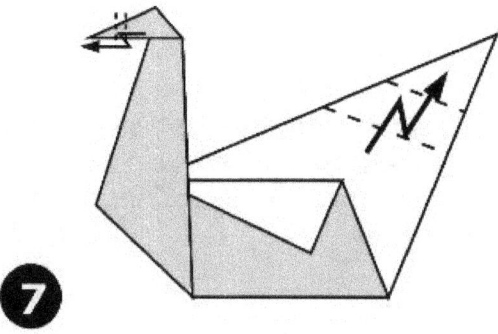

See the dotted lines at the tail? Fold down and inward along the dotted lines, doing a stair fold. Crease well. Fold the beak inwards slightly using a stair fold.

Step 8

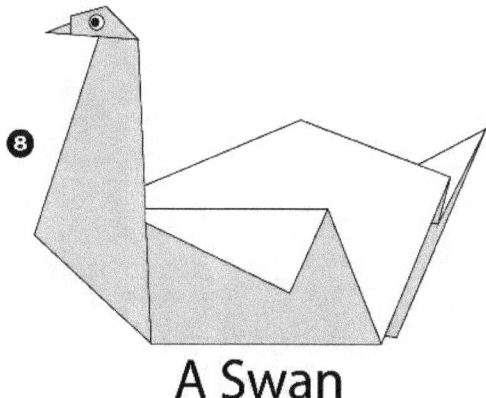

A Swan

Now you have an elegant swan! Just like the story of the ugly duckling transforming into a beautiful swan, you have transformed a regular sheet of paper into a special paper swan.

Fun Fact: Swans are the largest member of the duck and goose family. They have over 25,000 feathers. A male swan is called a cob, while a female swan is called a pen.

Did you know... In Mexico, candy wrappers are often weaved into handbags, jewelry, purses, and other accessories. This helps the environment by reusing paper that would normally be trash. It also helps the Mexican economy.

Chapter 18: Giraffe

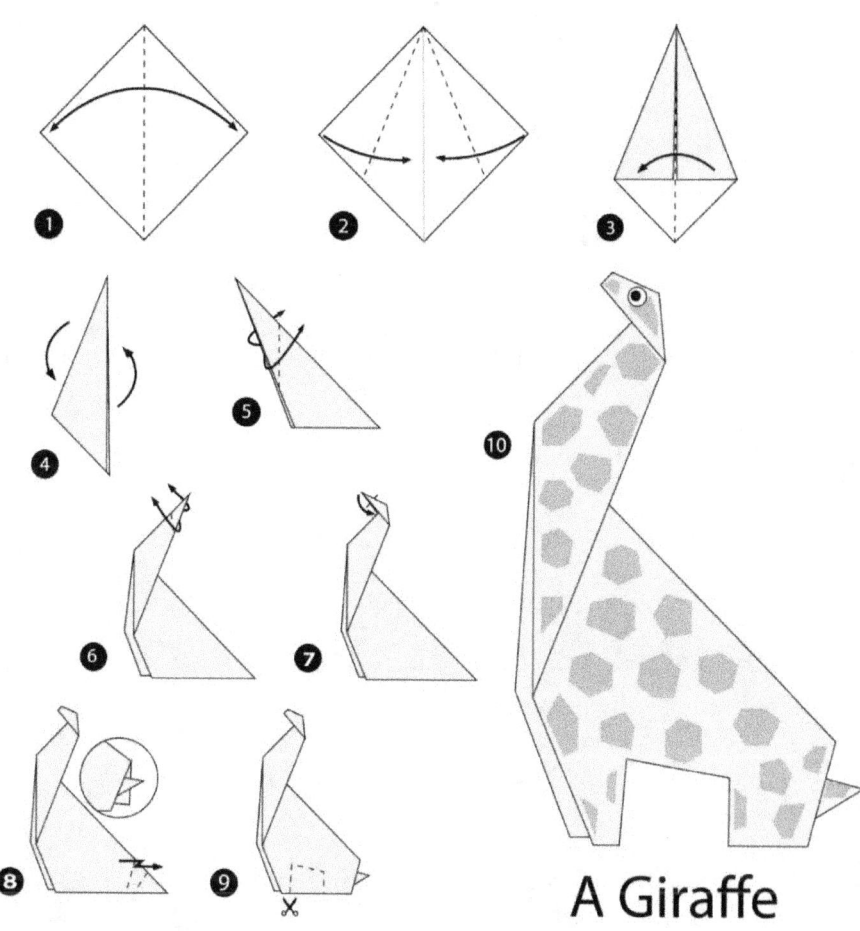

Our parade of animals continues with this cute giraffe. Like many of our other animal origami projects, start this one by placing your paper on a flat work surface with the color (or pattern) side down, and so that it is in the shape of a diamond.

Step 1

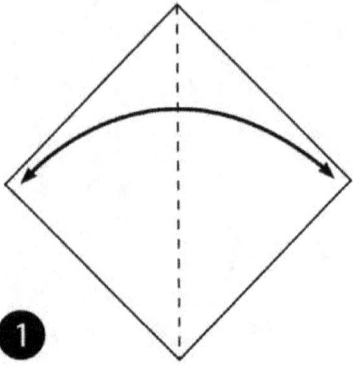

Fold the paper in half from left to right, crease well, and then unfold it again.

Step 2

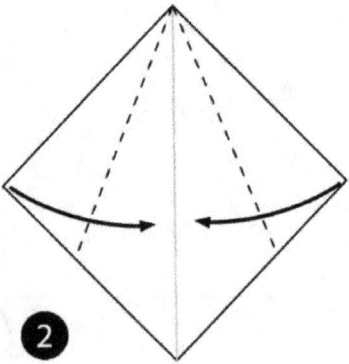

Following the dotted lines, fold the two outer corners in to meet at the center crease.

Step 3

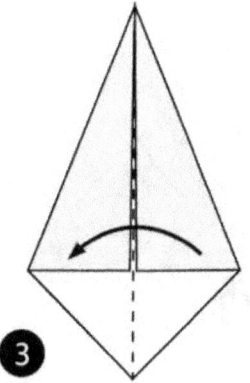

Now fold in half along the center line, as shown in the picture.

Step 4

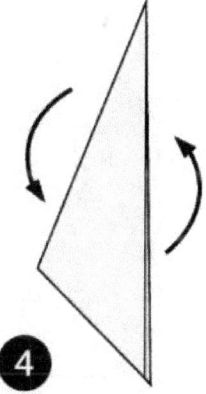

Turn the whole piece to the left, as shown, so that the top point is pointed up and to the left (like the picture).

Step 5

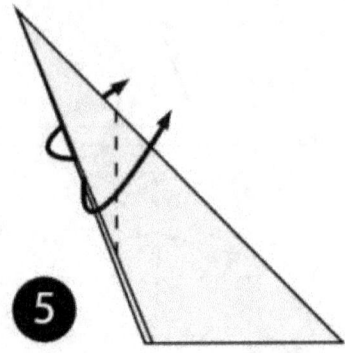

Following the arrows, fold the piece back and out, starting a hood fold.

Step 6

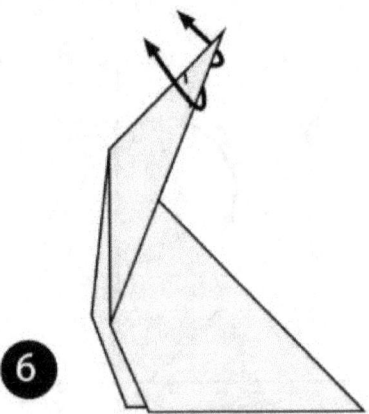

Complete the hood fold from above, creasing well.

Step 7

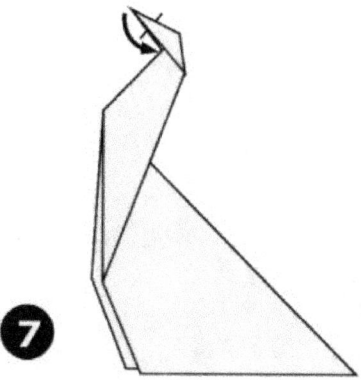

Now do a regular pocket fold on the very tip, folding inwards as shown.

Step 8

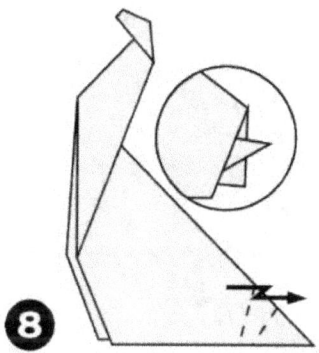

Perform a stair fold at the tail as shown in the image above.

Step 9

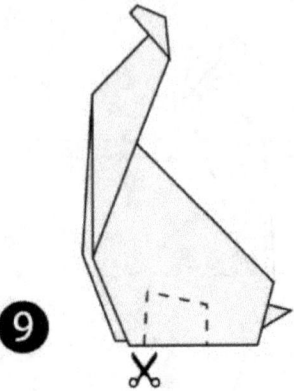

Ask an adult for some help with this part if you need to because it uses scissors. Cut along the dotted lines shown here, and remove the piece you cut out.

Step 10

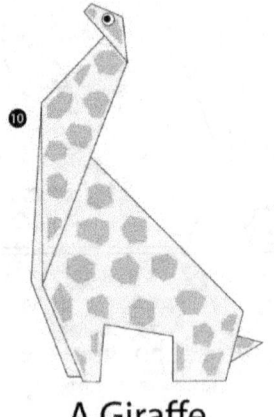

A Giraffe

Add eyes, and spots (or stripes, or stars, or whatever you want!), and your giraffe is all ready to play with the other animals.

Fun Fact: Giraffes are the tallest mammals on Earth. Their legs alone are taller than most people at about 6 feet tall. Even with their very long necks, their long legs actually make their neck and head unable to reach the ground when they bend forward.

Did you know... origami isn't just fun, it is also used for educational purposes. Folding origami can help better your understanding of geometry, visualization skills, learning fractions in math, and problem solving, just to name a few!

Chapter 19: Squirrel

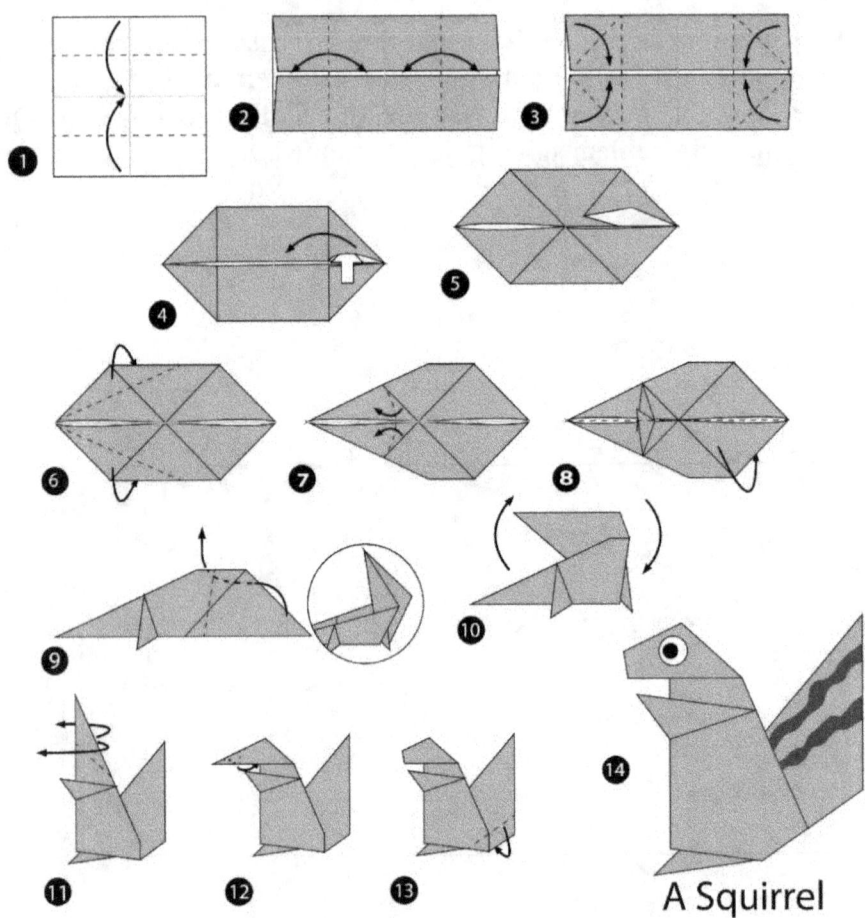

A Squirrel

For our last animal buddy, we have a little squirrel. Start with your paper flat on your work surface, color (or pattern) side down, in the shape of a square. Prepare your paper by folding in half from top to bottom, and from left to right, and unfold. Use these creases as a guide.

Step 1

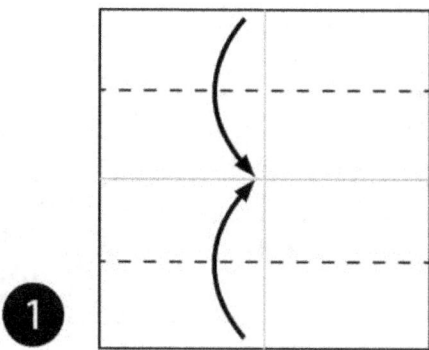

Fold the top edge down to the center crease. Fold the bottom edge up to the center crease, meeting with the top edge in the middle. Crease well.

Step 2

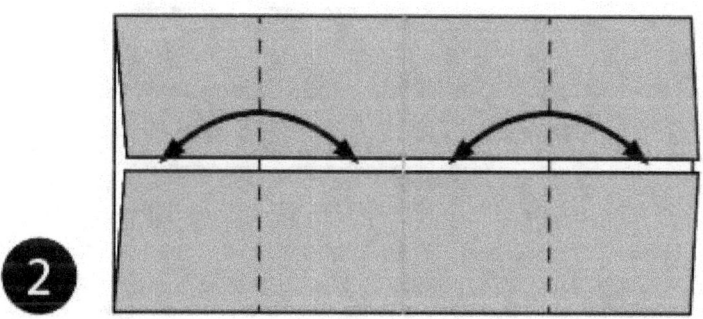

Fold the left edge in order to meet the center crease. Then fold the right in to the center crease as well, meeting with the left edge. Crease well, and unfold again.

Step 3

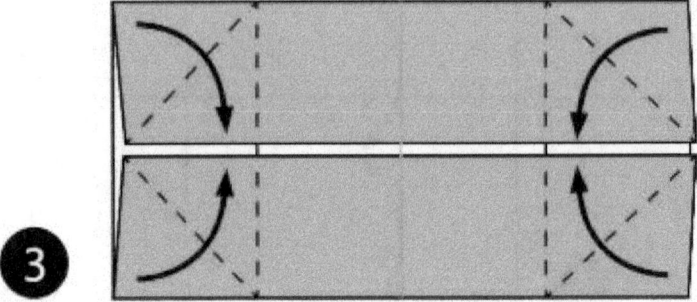

Fold the top left corner down to the center line as shown in the picture. Do the same thing on the other three remaining corners.

Step 4

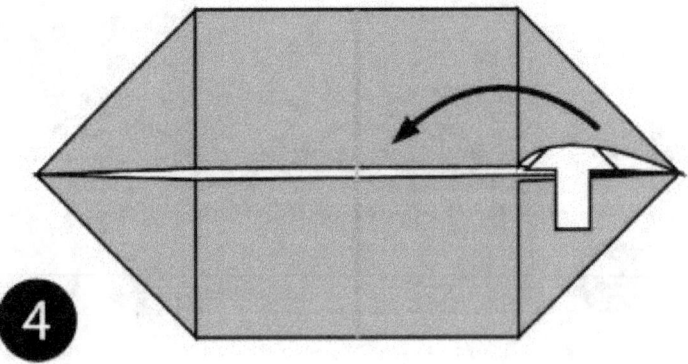

You should now have a pocket where the white arrow is. Lift it open and flatten it with a squash fold.

Step 5

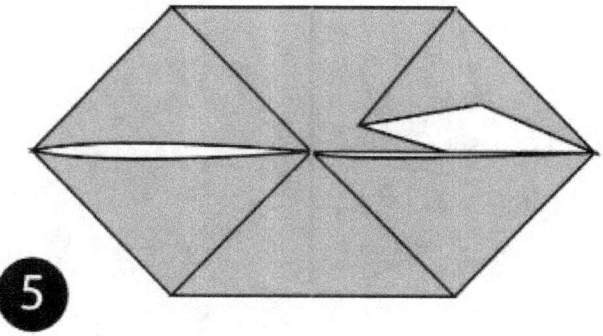

Repeat step four on the three remaining pockets, as shown.

Step 6

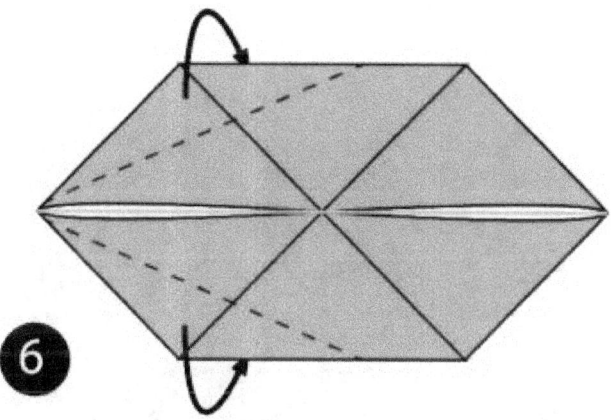

Following the dotted lines, fold these two sections backwards with a mountain fold.

Step 7

251

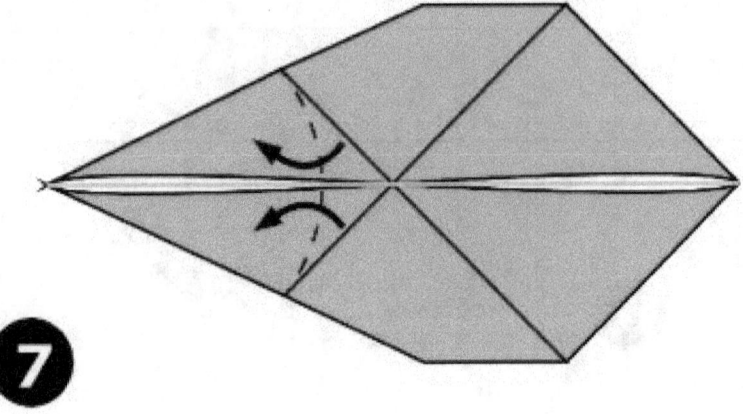

See the dotted lines and arrows? Fold inward along the dotted lines, so that these areas are being tucked in.

Step 8

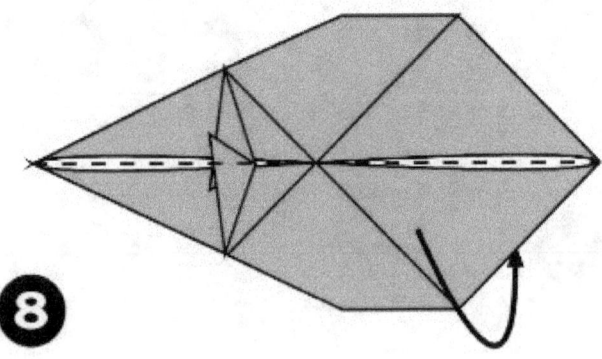

Fold in half by tucking the bottom part behind with a mountain fold, as shown by the arrow.

Step 9

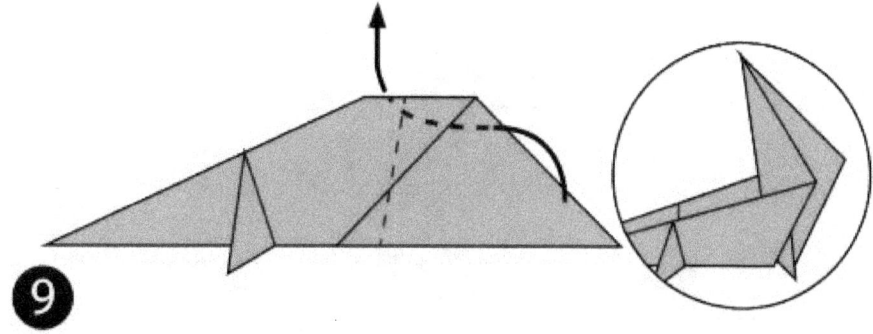

Follow the dotted lines, and fold inward, tucking in, using a pocket fold.

Step 10

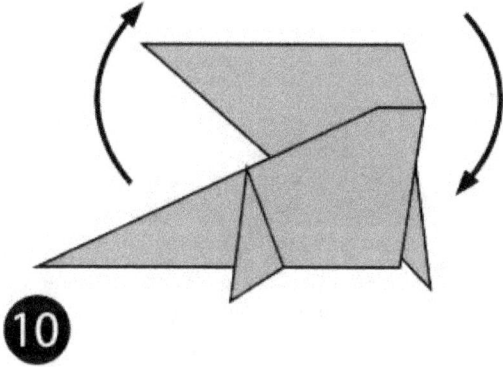

Rotate the piece a bit to the right, so that the points on the left are now at the top.

Step 11

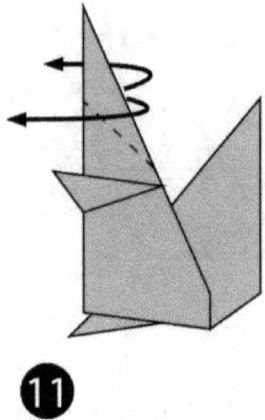

This part is tricky, but you can do it! Fold along the dotted line, going inward and tucking, and then flattening out. This is the hood fold again.

Step 12

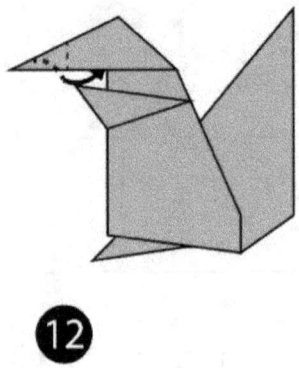

Now use an inward fold where the dotted line is, tucking the point inside.

Step 13

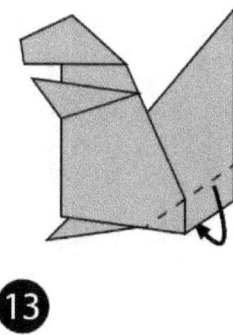

See the dotted line? Fold along the dotted line, folding the edge up inside.

Step 14

A Squirrel

Fantastic! Add an eye, some nose details, some whiskers, and anything else you'd like to make your squirrel unique.

Fun Fact: A newborn squirrel is only about one inch long!

Did you know... According to an ancient Japanese legend, if you fold one thousand cranes you will be granted a wish. What do you think? Is this legend true? Why or why not?

See You Soon!

You made it to the end! Like all good things, this adventure must come to an end. But don't worry! There are many more adventures ahead of you. If you haven't already, maybe you'd like to join me for the adventure that started this series, my first book: *"Origami for Kids: Easy Japanese Origami Instruction Book for Kids."* There are all kinds of neat things in it that you can learn to fold!

We saw a lot of animals in this adventure. Did you also find any treasure while reading this book? What did you learn or discover as you made your way through? There are lots of fun and surprising facts about both animals and origami throughout this book. Did you get to read them all? I hope so! If not, take some time to go back and read a bit more. You may learn something really interesting, or discover something entirely new to you!

Maybe you discovered a true passion for origami. Maybe you found you love animal prints, or are interested in a specific kind of animal and would like to learn more about it. Maybe you simply discovered a love for reading and learning in a way you didn't know of before. Or maybe you had a good time, and now you're going to move on to a whole new experience. Whatever the case may be, I hope you enjoyed this journey!

You can make just about anything from paper. A paper cup, pretty gift boxes, wrappers, hopping frogs, coin purses, wallets, the options go on and on.

If you had fun and enjoyed yourself throughout this book, please let me know by leaving a review on Amazon. I'd love to hear your thoughts!

Thank you!

www.ingramcontent.com/pod-product-compliance
Lightning Source LLC
Chambersburg PA
CBHW071227080526
44587CB00013BA/1528